The View from There

The art of Hugh McDonnold

ISBN: 0982903839
ISBN-13: 978-0982903834

CONTENTS

1. buildings…

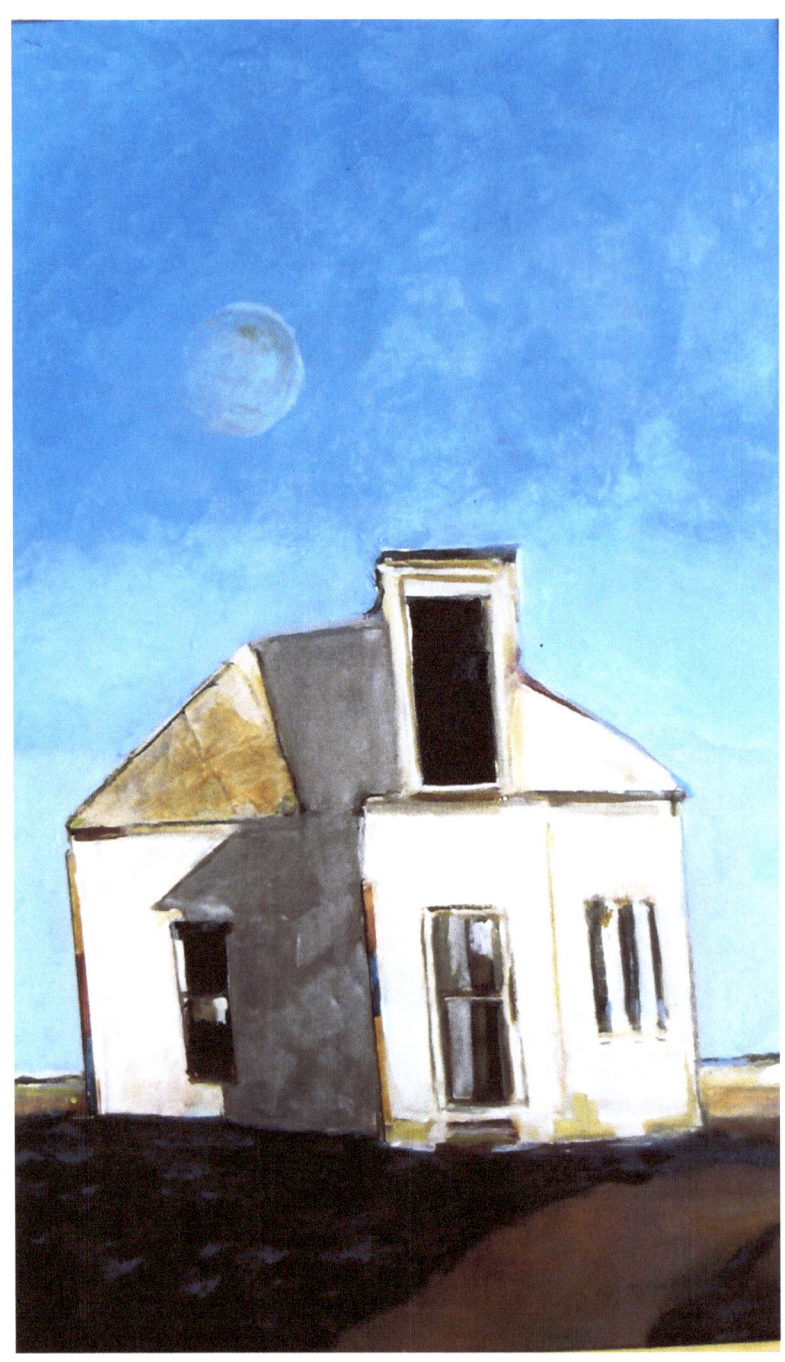

Without a Dream in My Heart, 2005, acrylic/oil on canvas

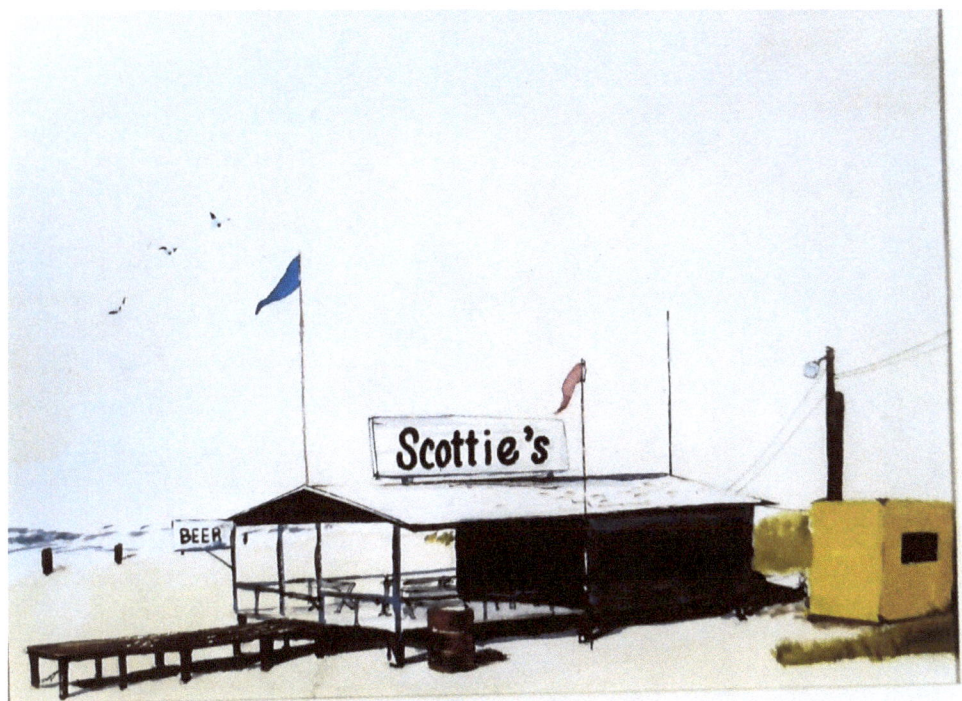

Beachfront Dining, circa 1987, watercolor on paper

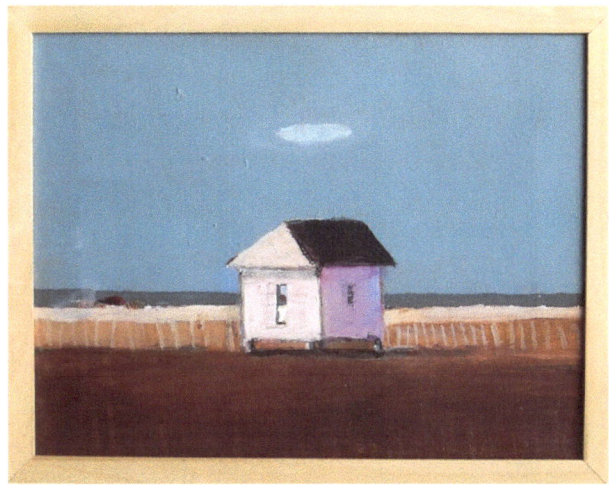

Little House with Cloud 2, circa 2005, acrylic on canvas

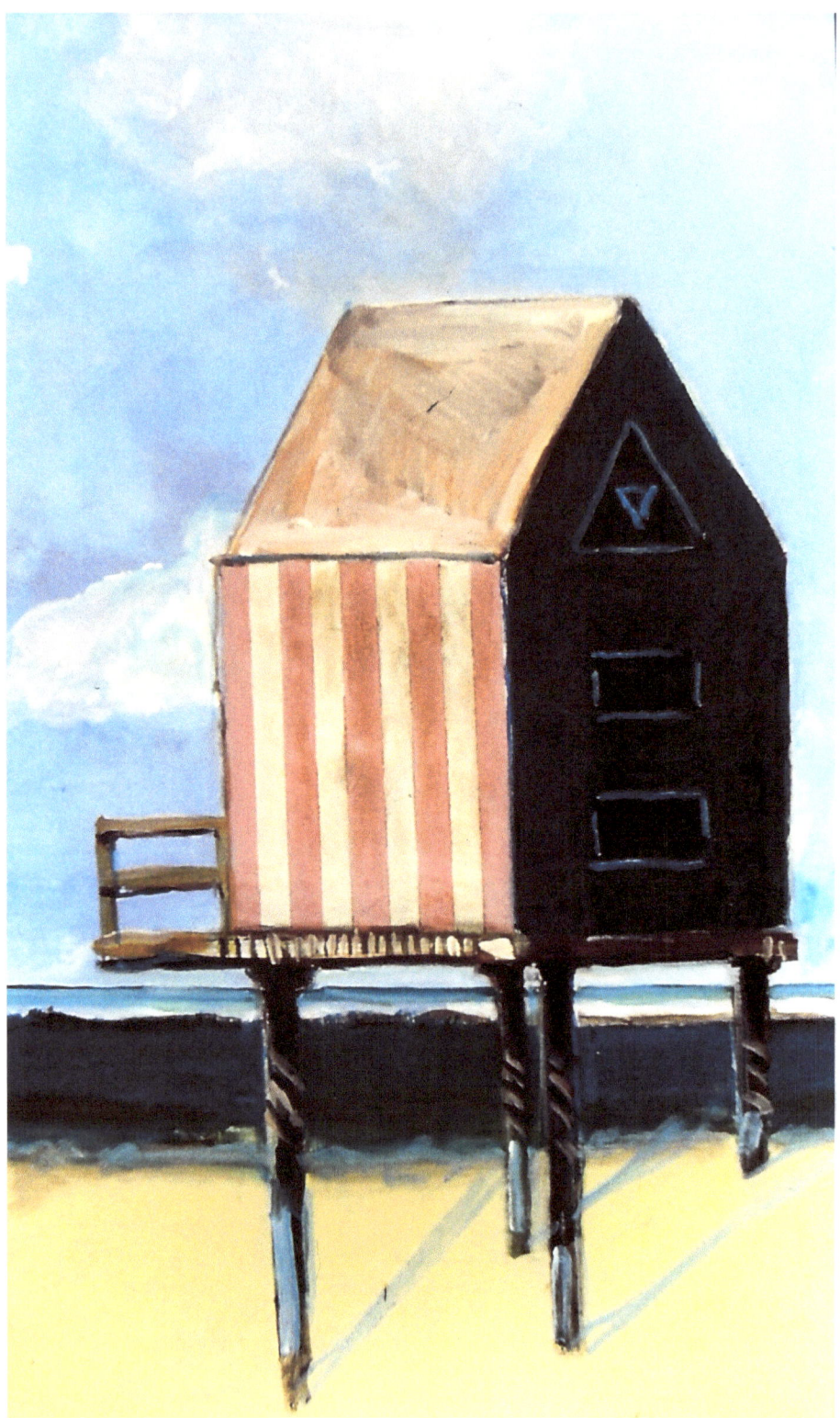

Julie's House, 2003, acrylic on canvas

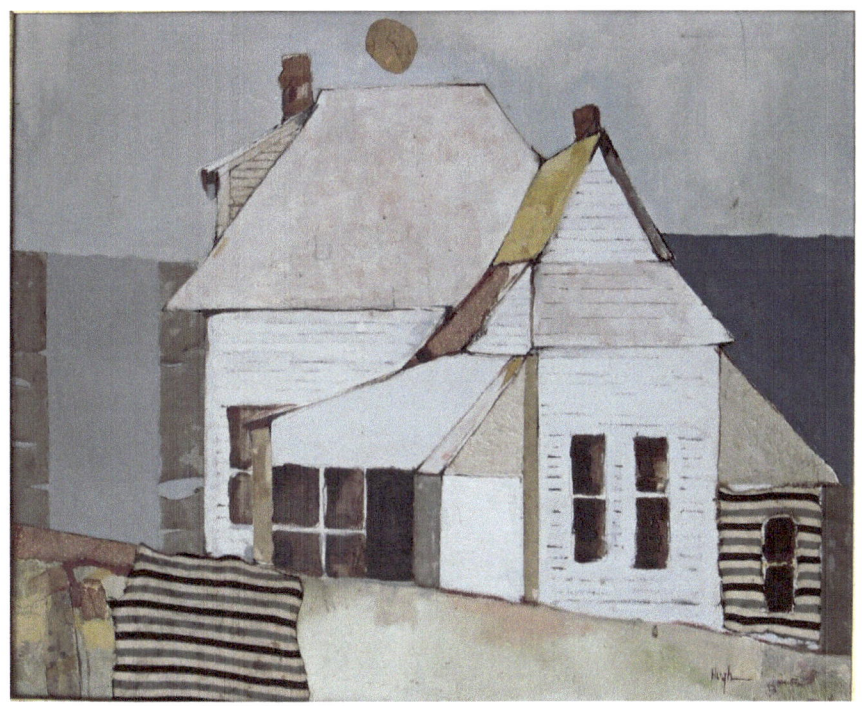

Country House, circa 1971, mixed media

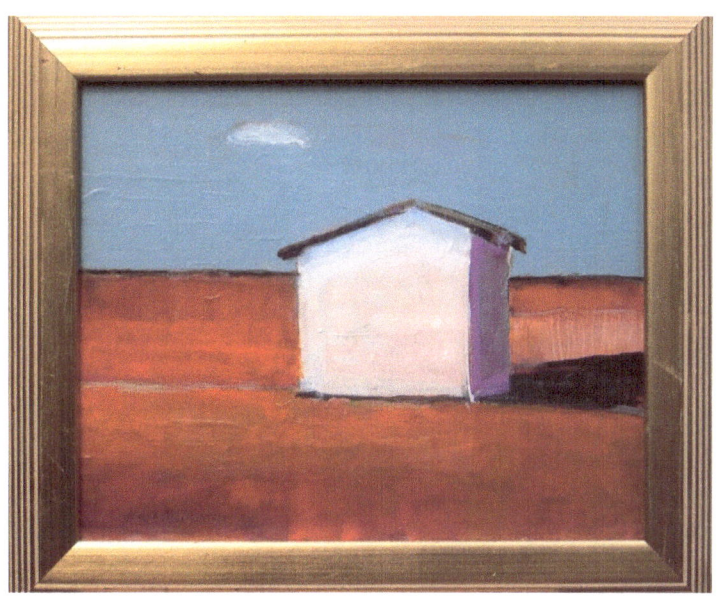

Little House with Cloud 1, circa 2005, oil on canvas

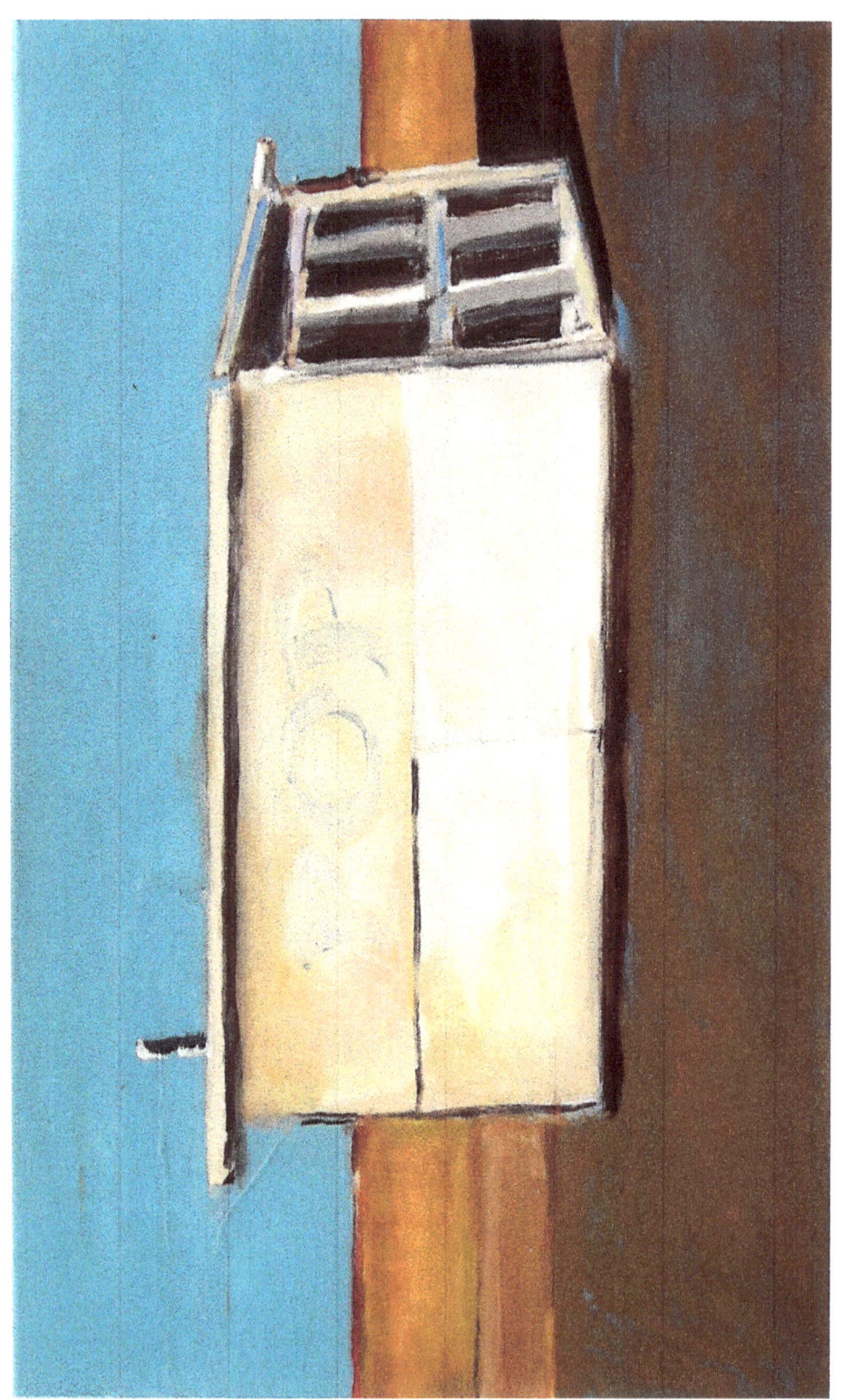

New Year's Eve, 2006, acrylic on canvas

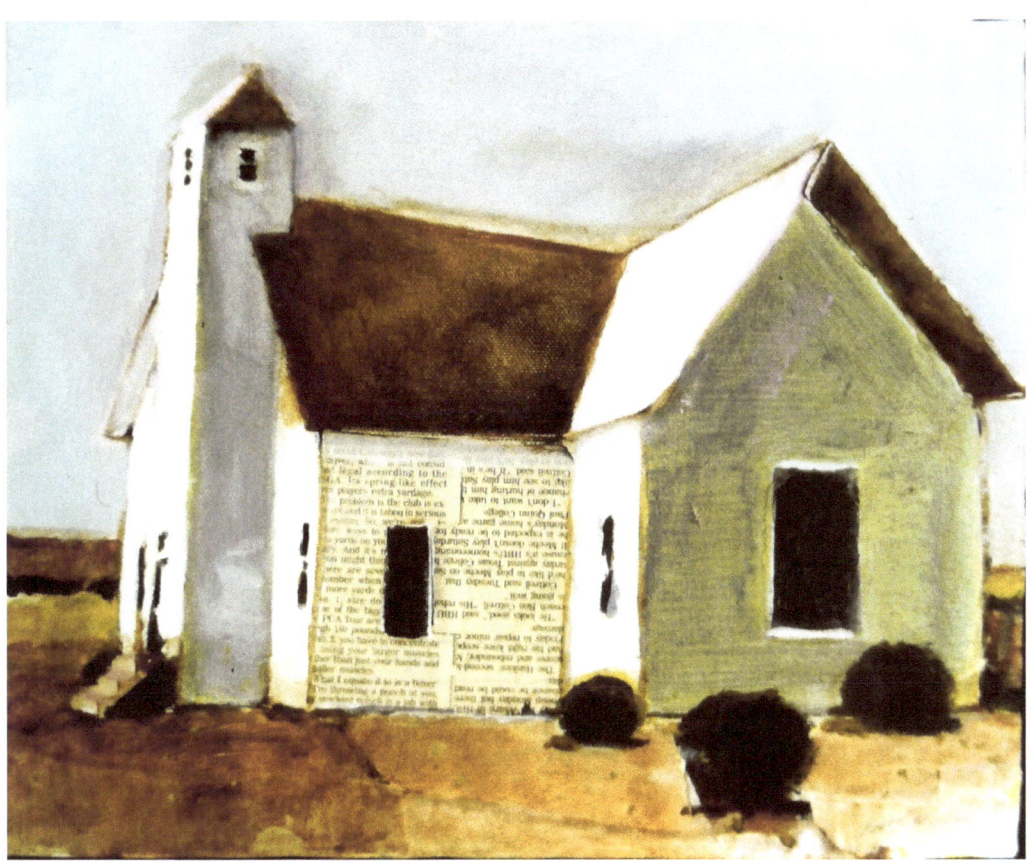

Church, date unknown, mixed media

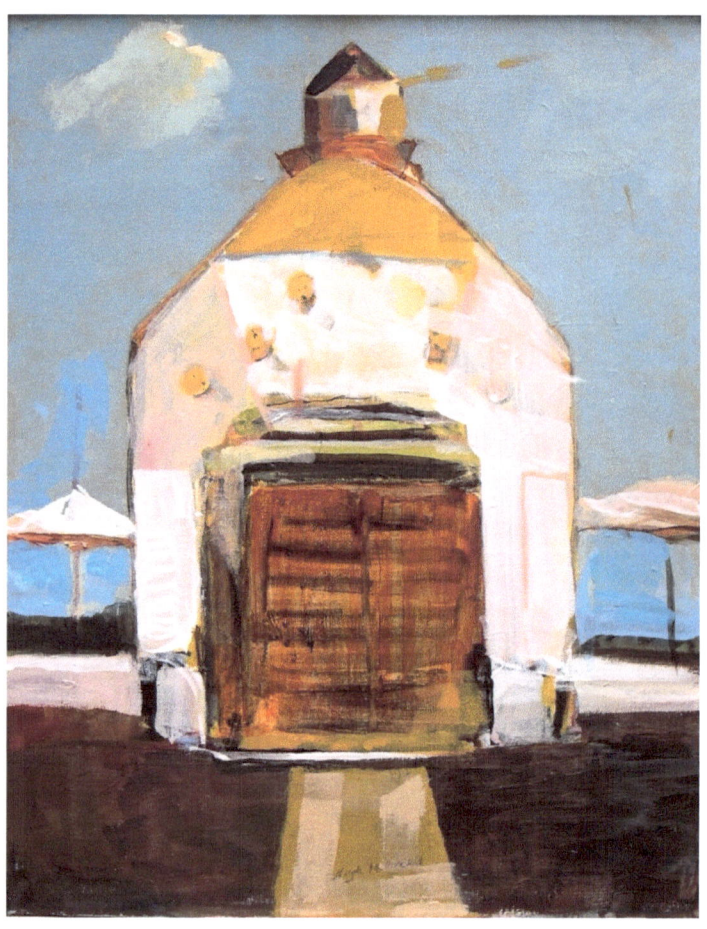

Juke Box, 2005, acrylic on canvas

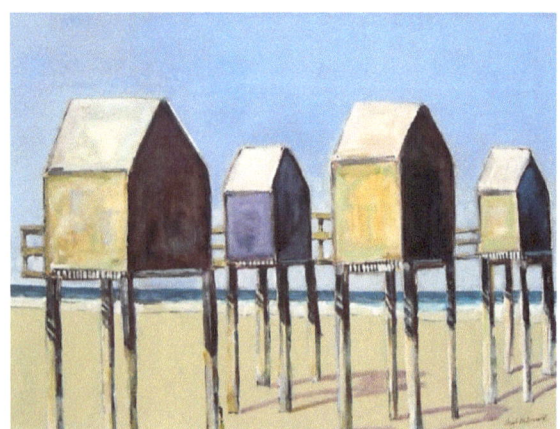

Four Standing, circa 2003, acrylic on canvas

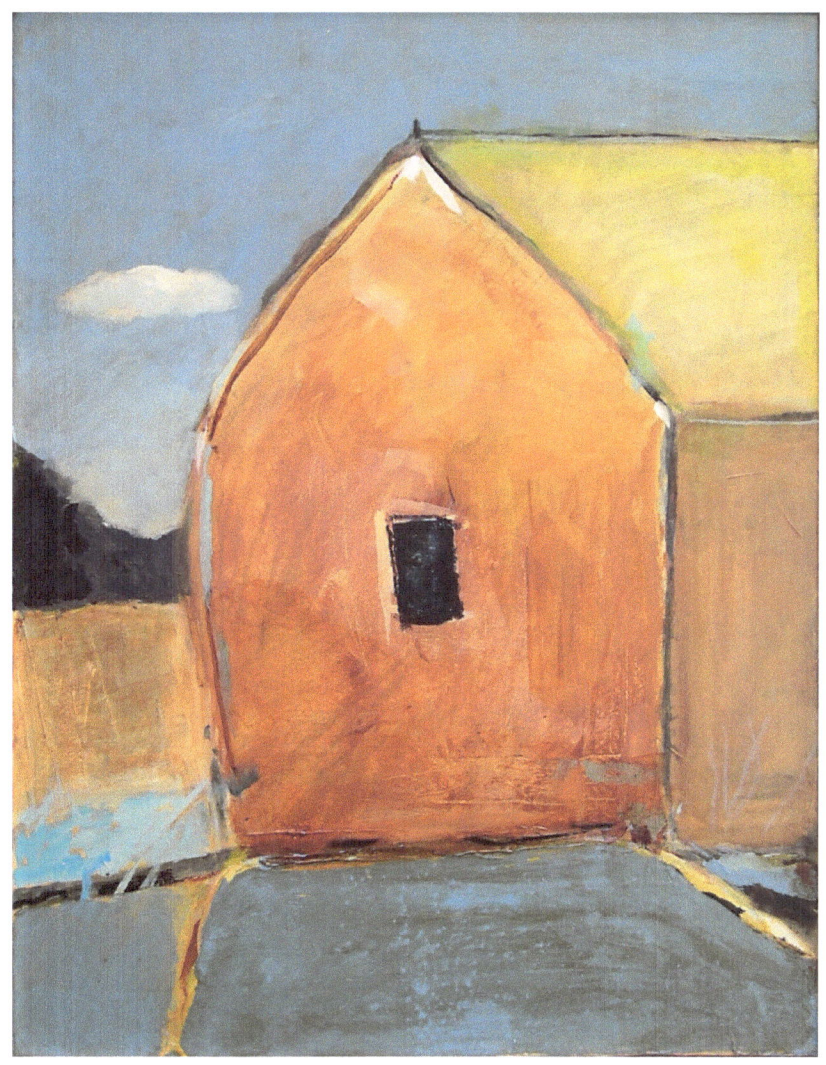

Cricket and the Cloud, 2000-2005, acrylic on canvas

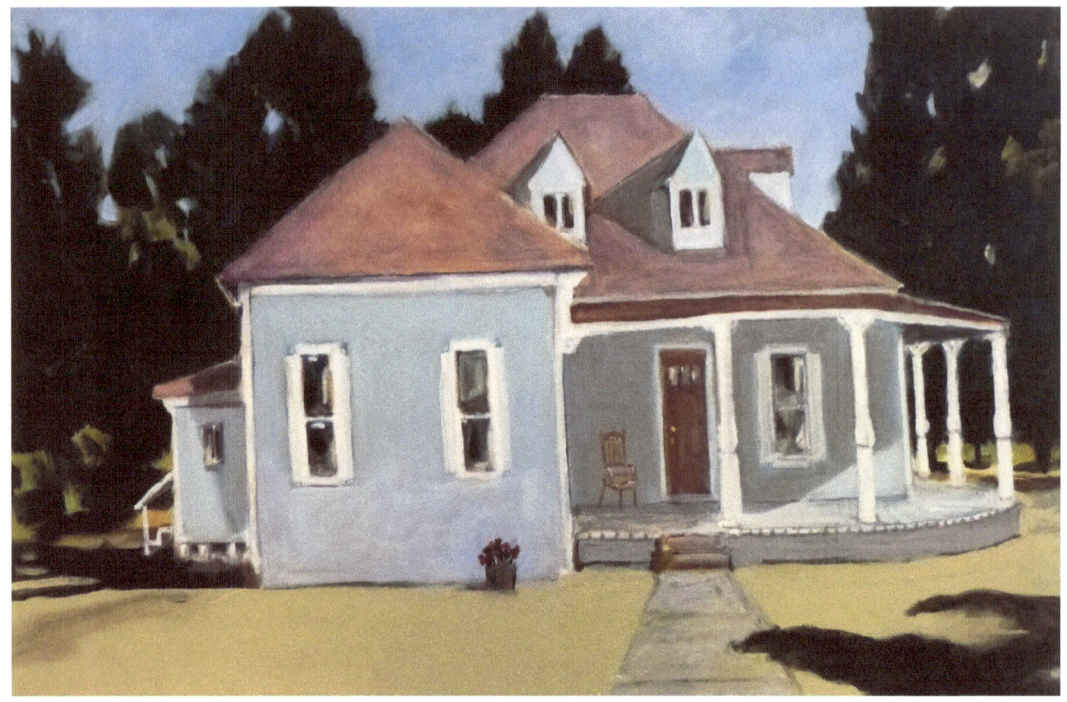

Marilyn's House, circa 1999, acrylic on canvas

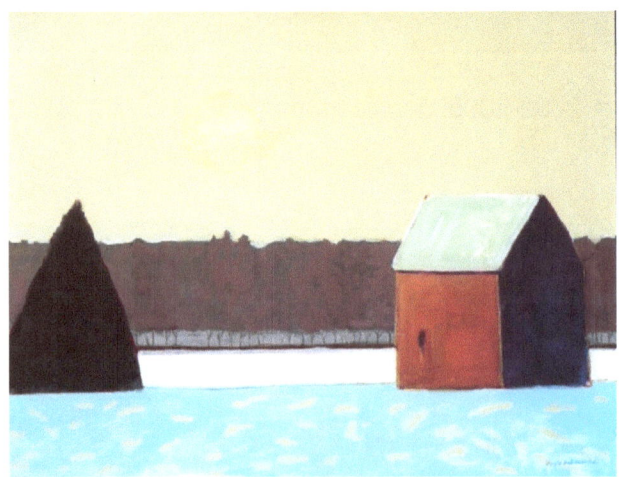

Frozen, 1995-2000, acrylic on canvas

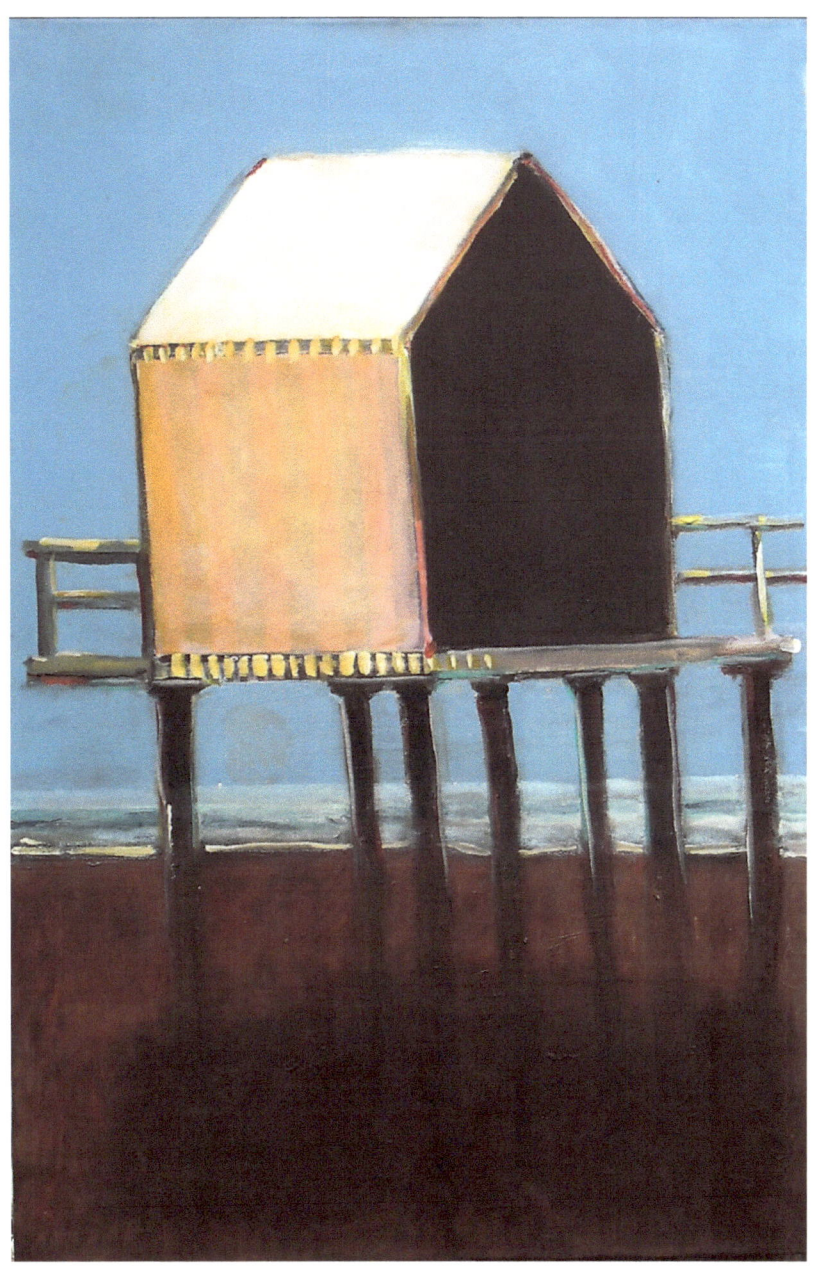

Moonlight House, 2000-2005, acrylic on canvas

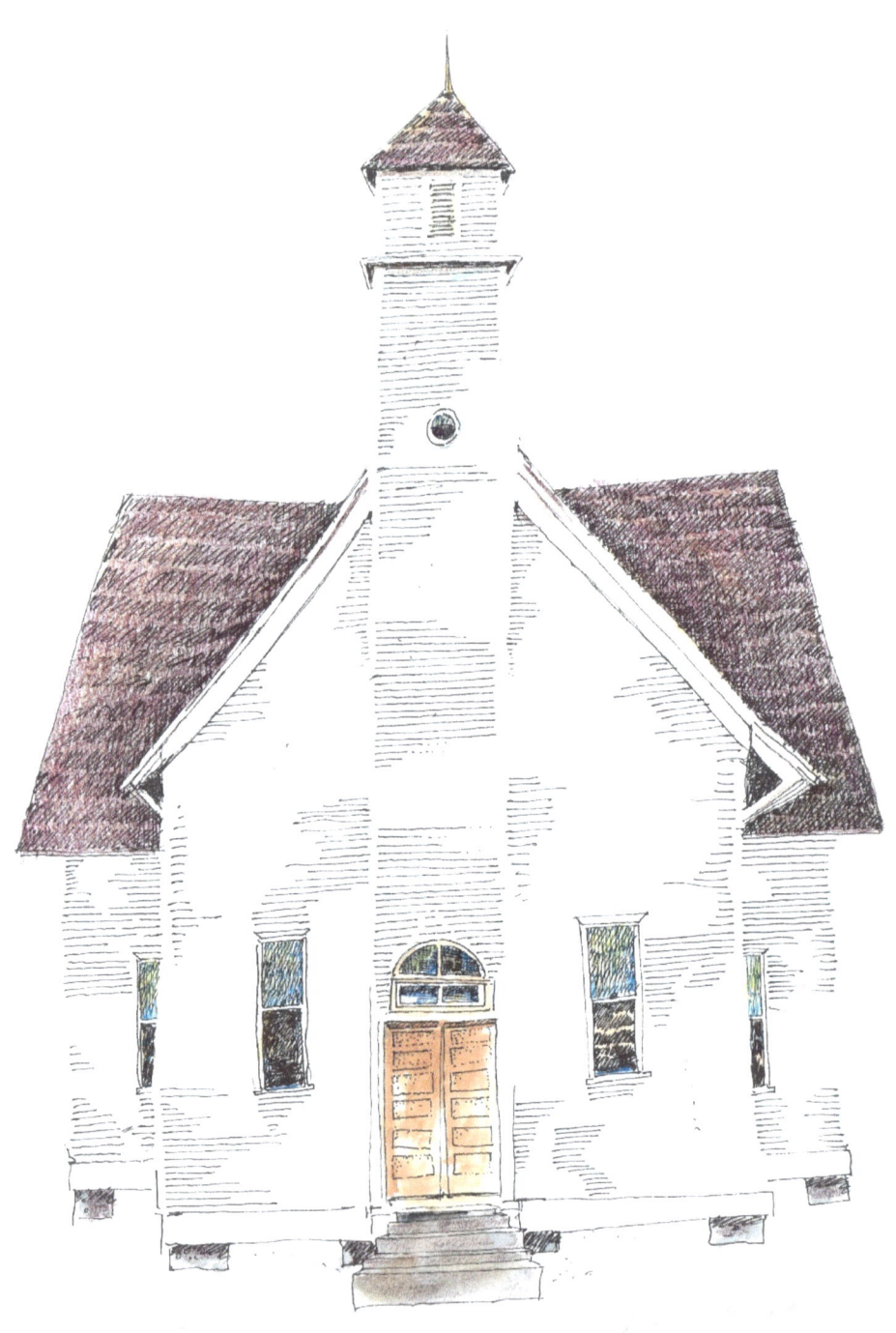

Church, 2000, ink and colored pencil

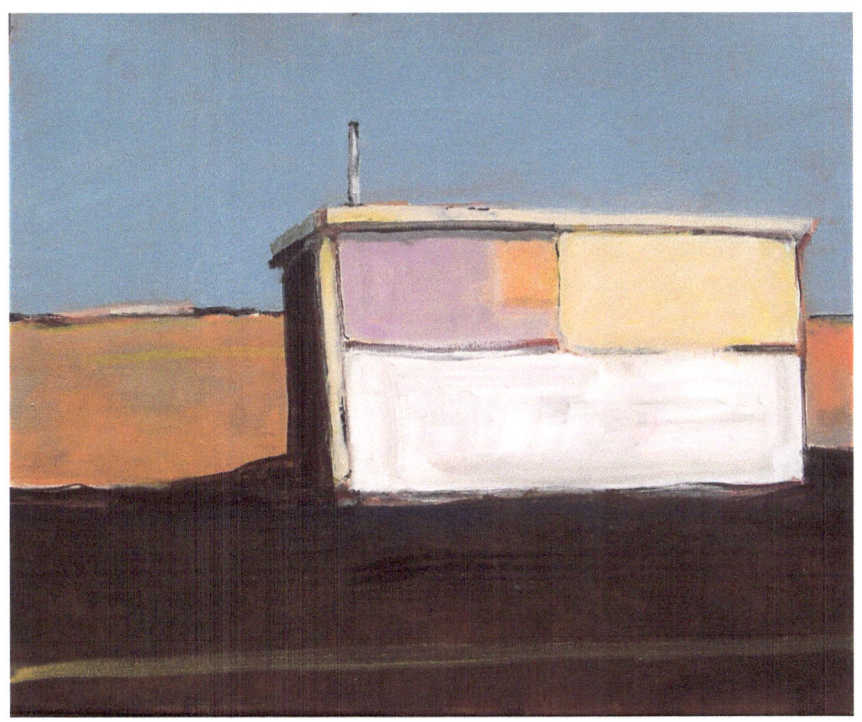

Fireworks Stand, 2006, acrylic on canvas

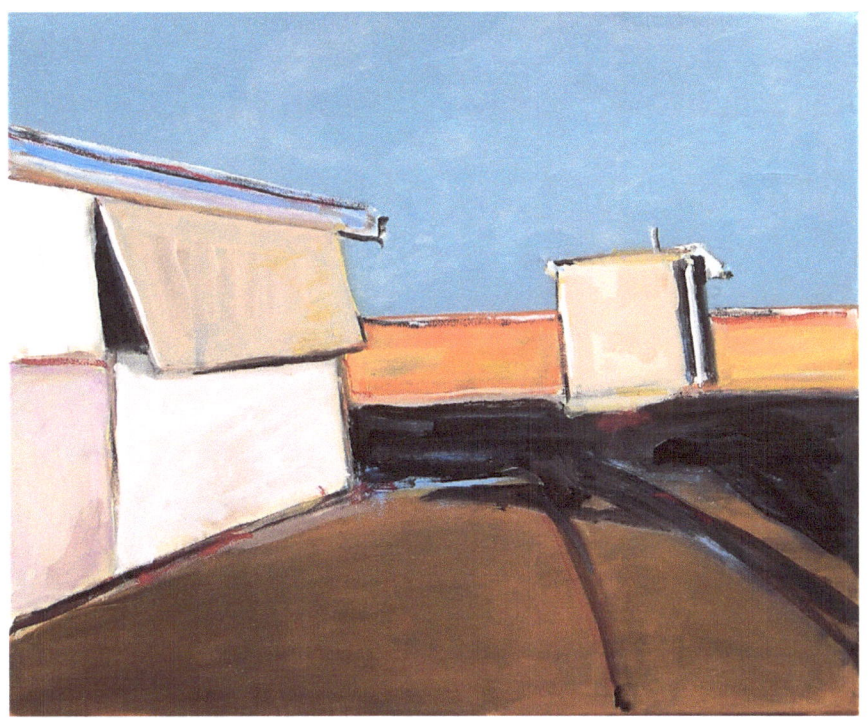

Fireworks Stand 2, 2006, acrylic on canvas

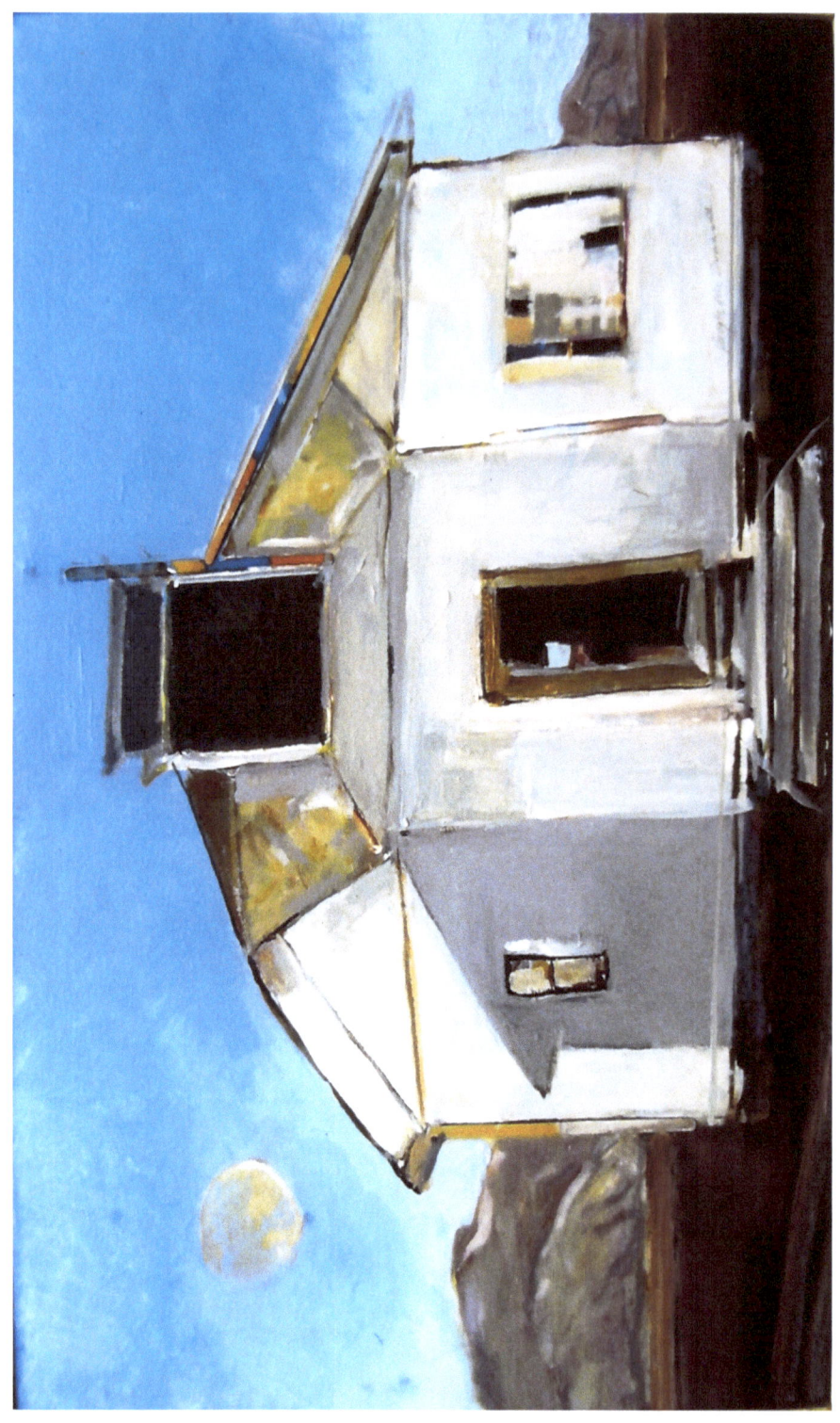

You Left Me Standing Alone, 2005, acrylic on canvas

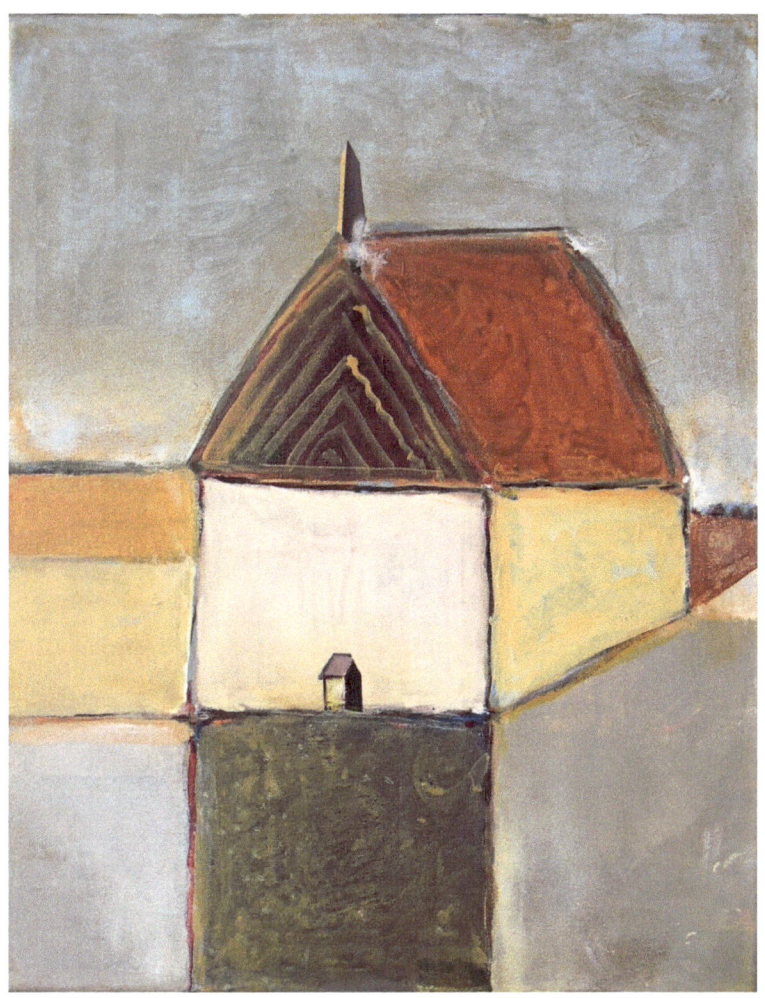

House on the Block, circa 2005, acrylic on canvas

Country Church, 1966, oil on canvas

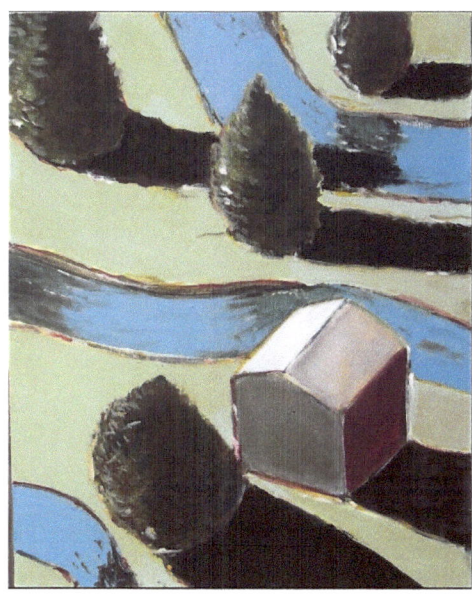

Seattle Aerial, circa 2003, oil on canvas

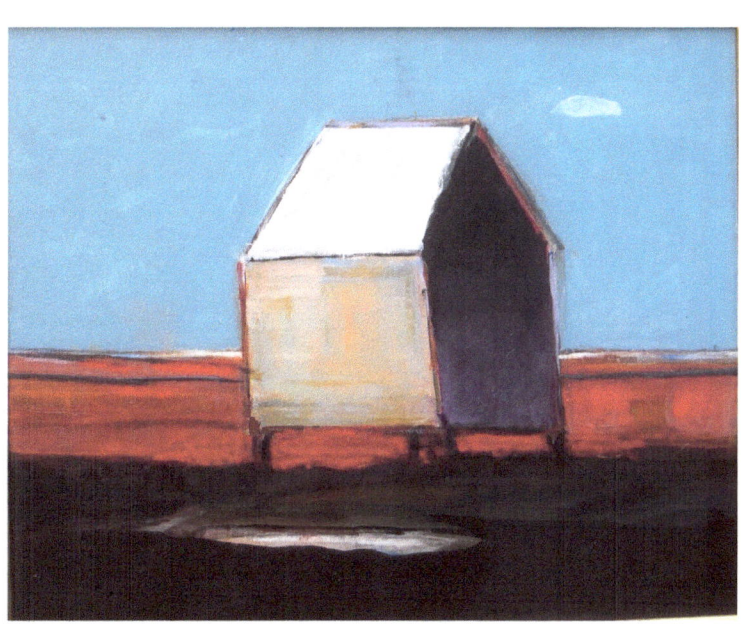

Little House with Cloud, circa 2005, acrylic on canvas

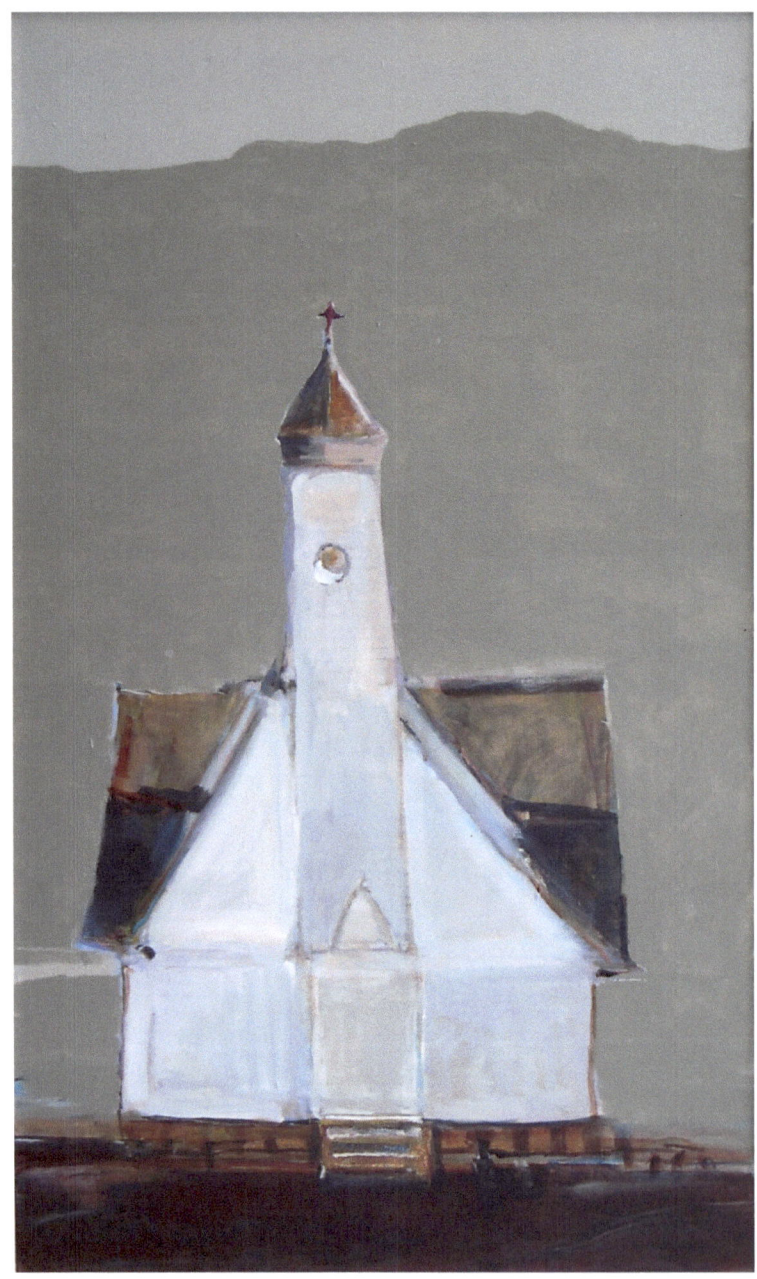

White Church, 1998, acrylic on canvas

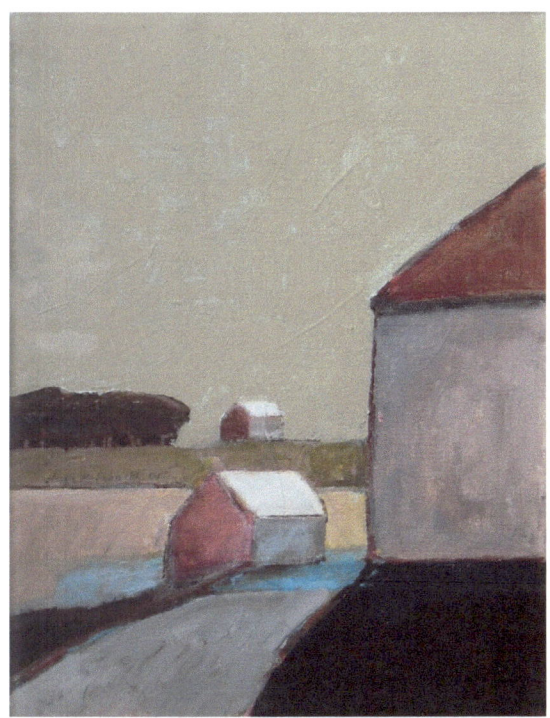

Venetian Red, 2000-2005, acrylic on canvas

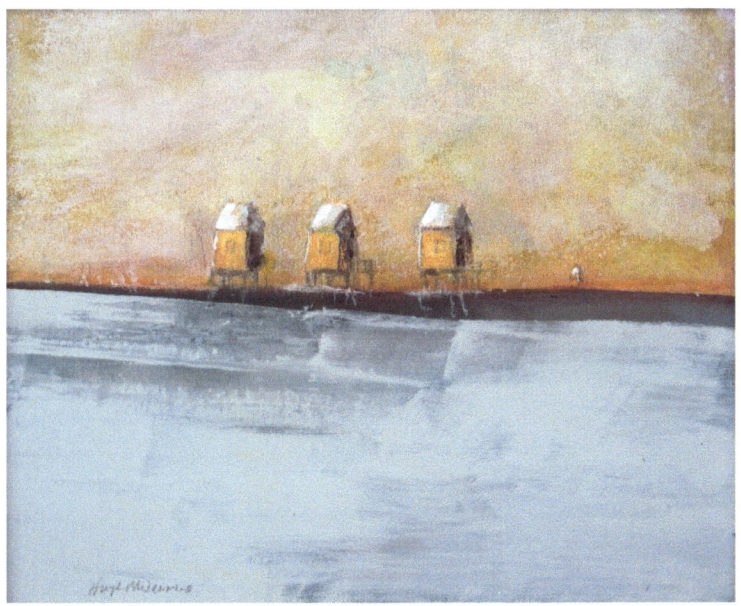

Three Houses, circa 2005, acrylic on canvas

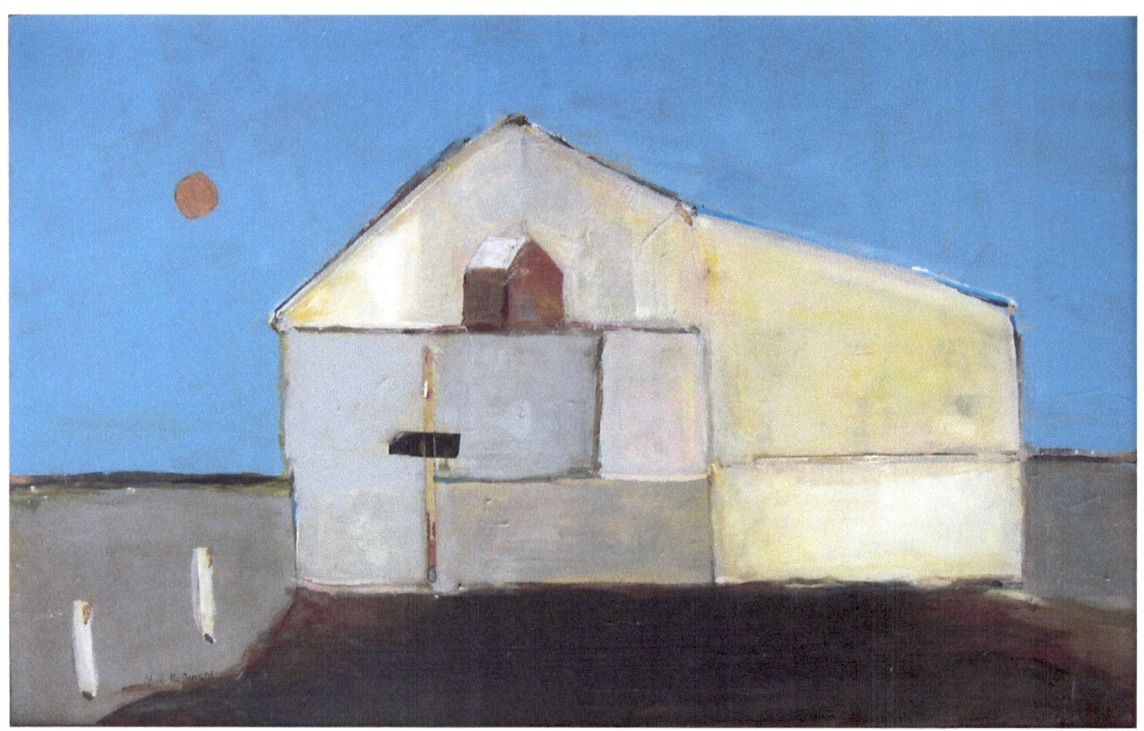

Trinity Tide, circa 2005, acrylic on canvas

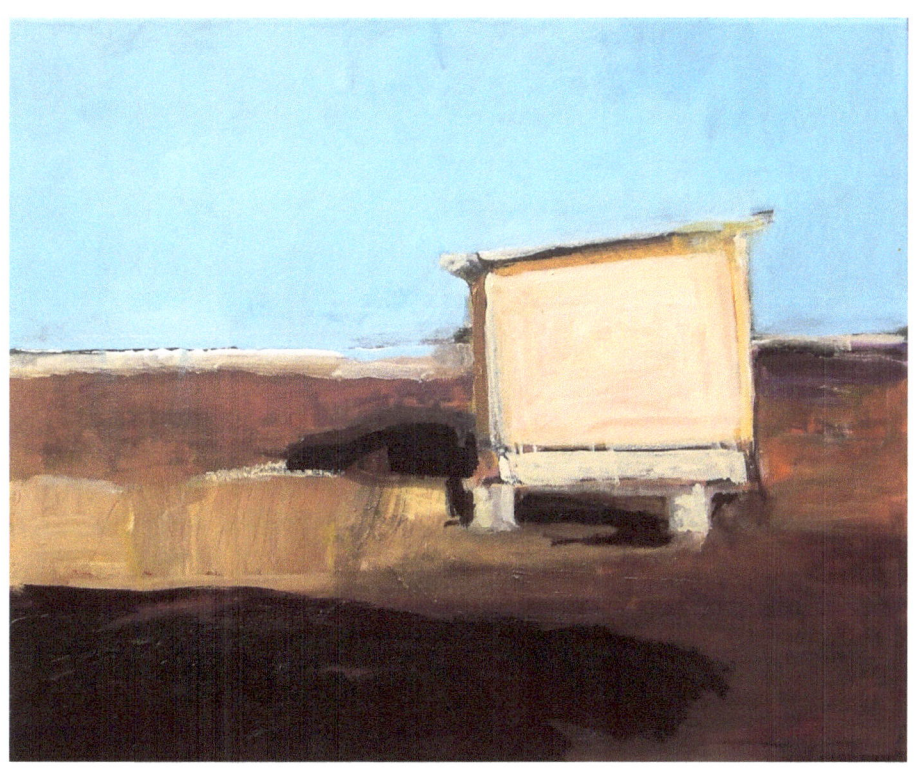

Frances' House, circa 2005, acrylic on canvas

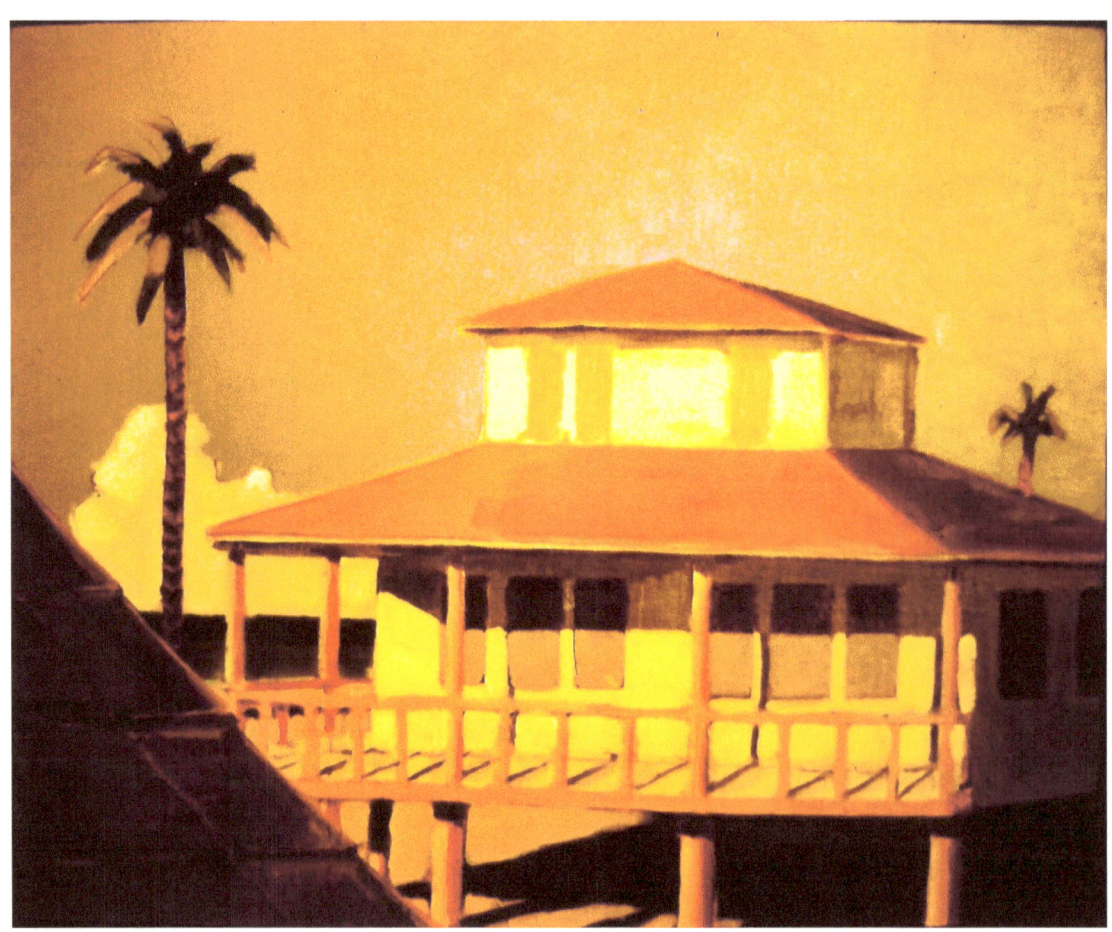

Obstructed View, circa 1989, acrylic on canvas

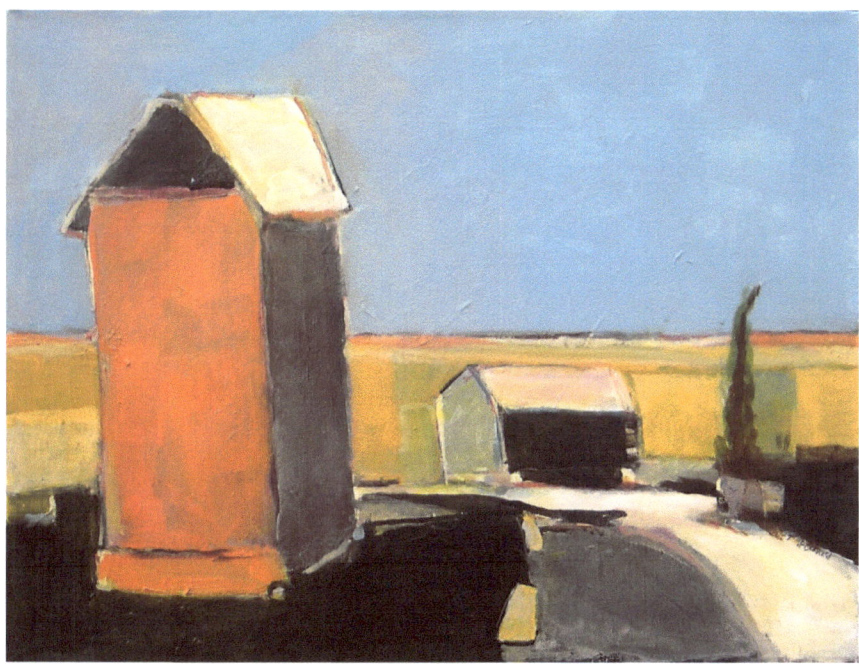

Route 66, circa 2003, acrylic on canvas

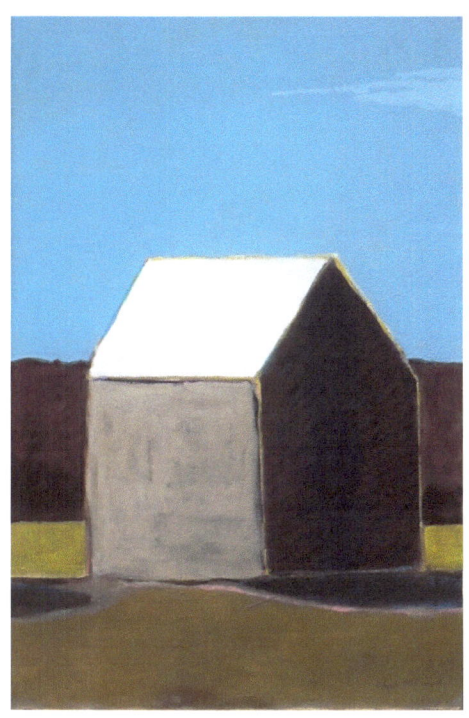

Richard's House, circa 2005, acrylic on canvas

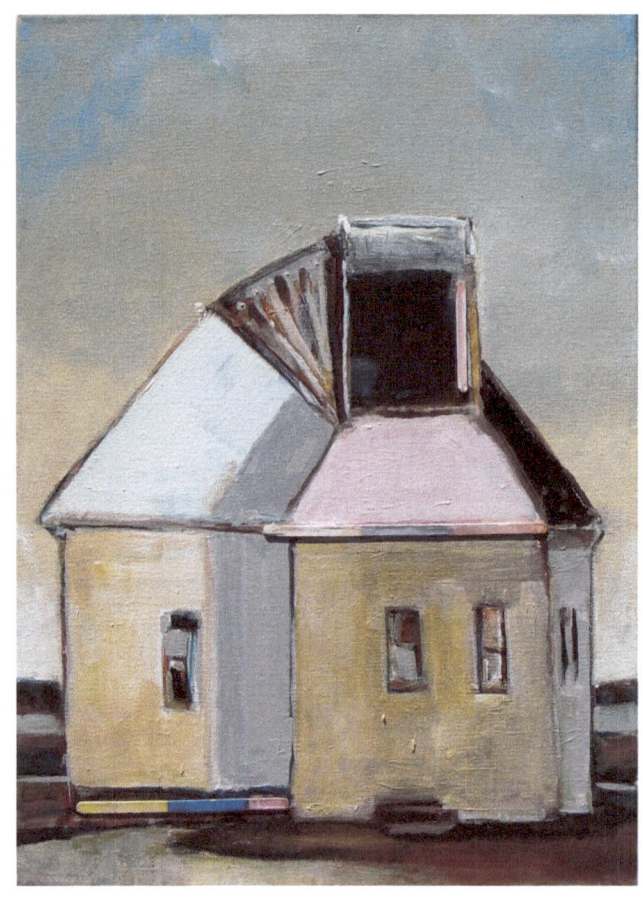

New Mexico House, circa 2002, acrylic on canvas

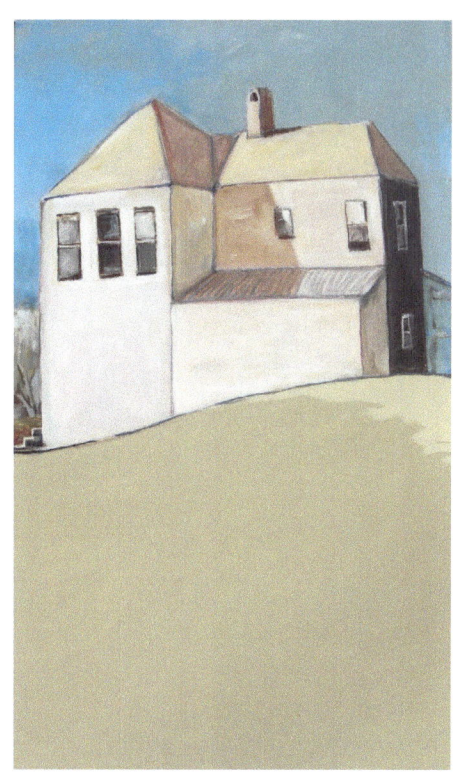

Halfway House, circa 1999, acrylic on canvas

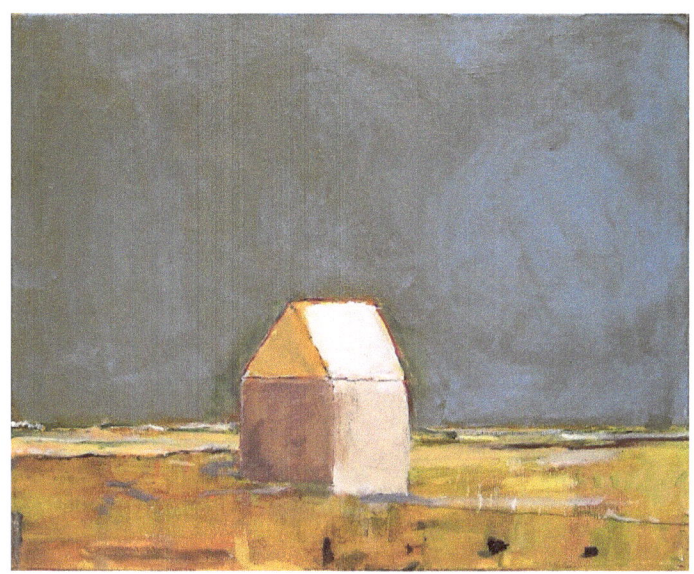

Beachcomber, circa 2005, acrylic on canvas

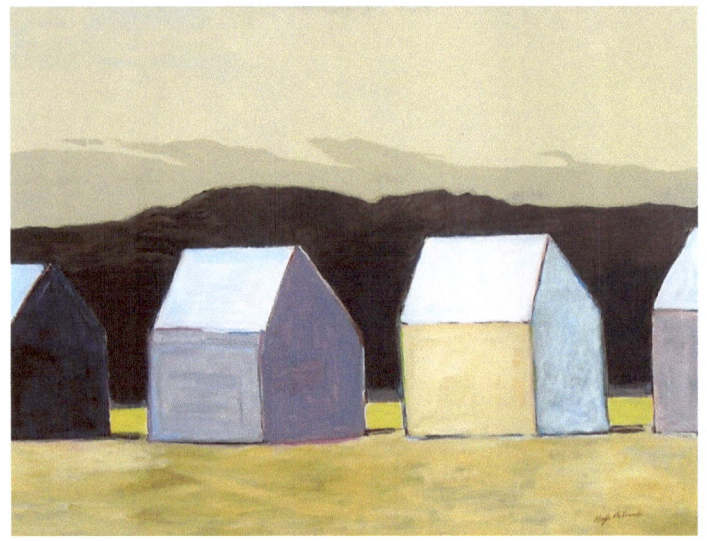

Camp Huaco, 2000-2005, acrylic on canvas

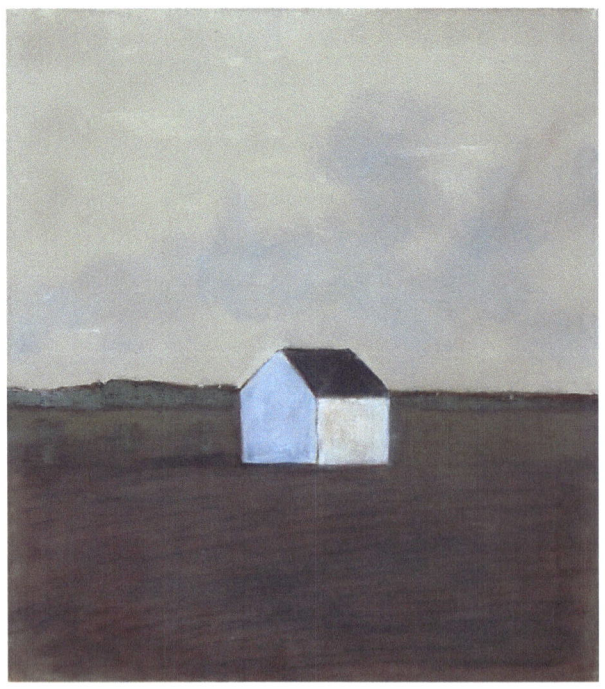

Center House, 2000-2005, acrylic on canvas

2. people…

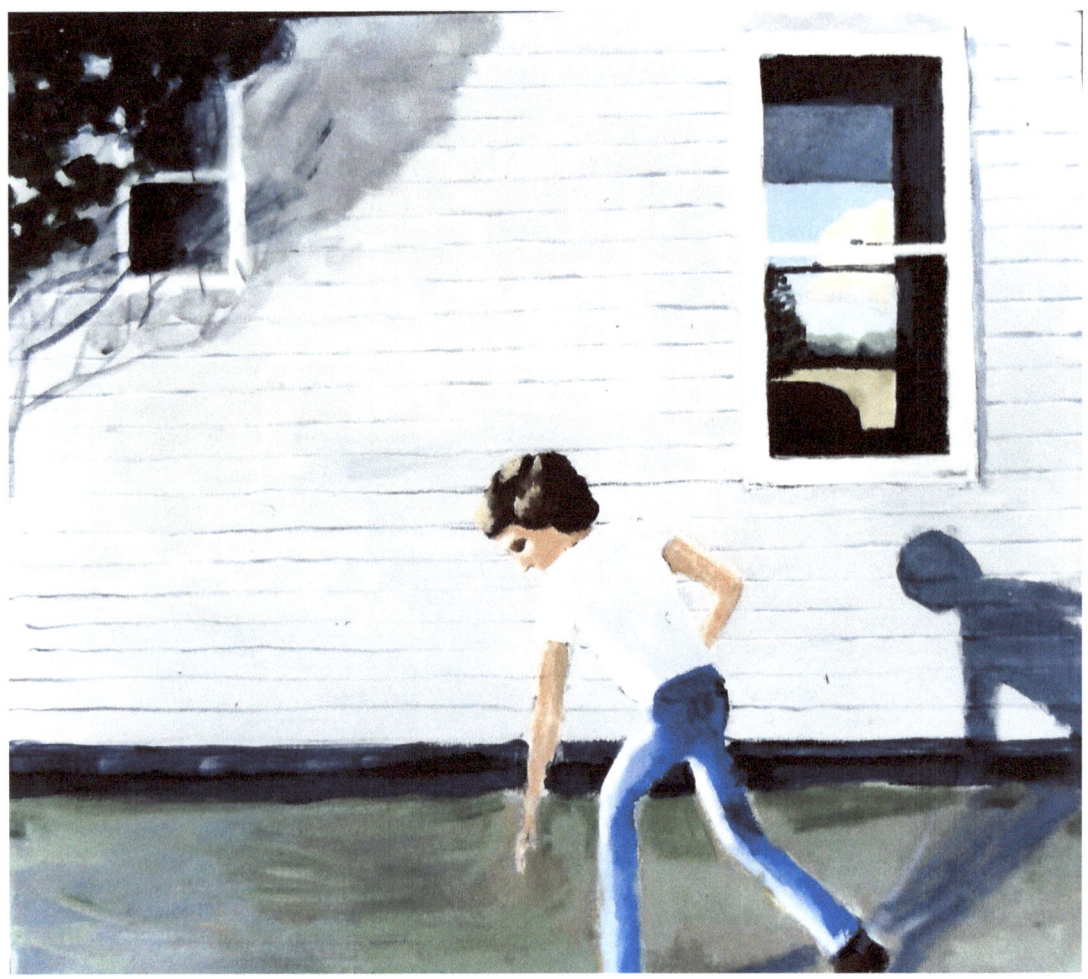

Saturday Afternoon, circa 1975, acrylic on canvas

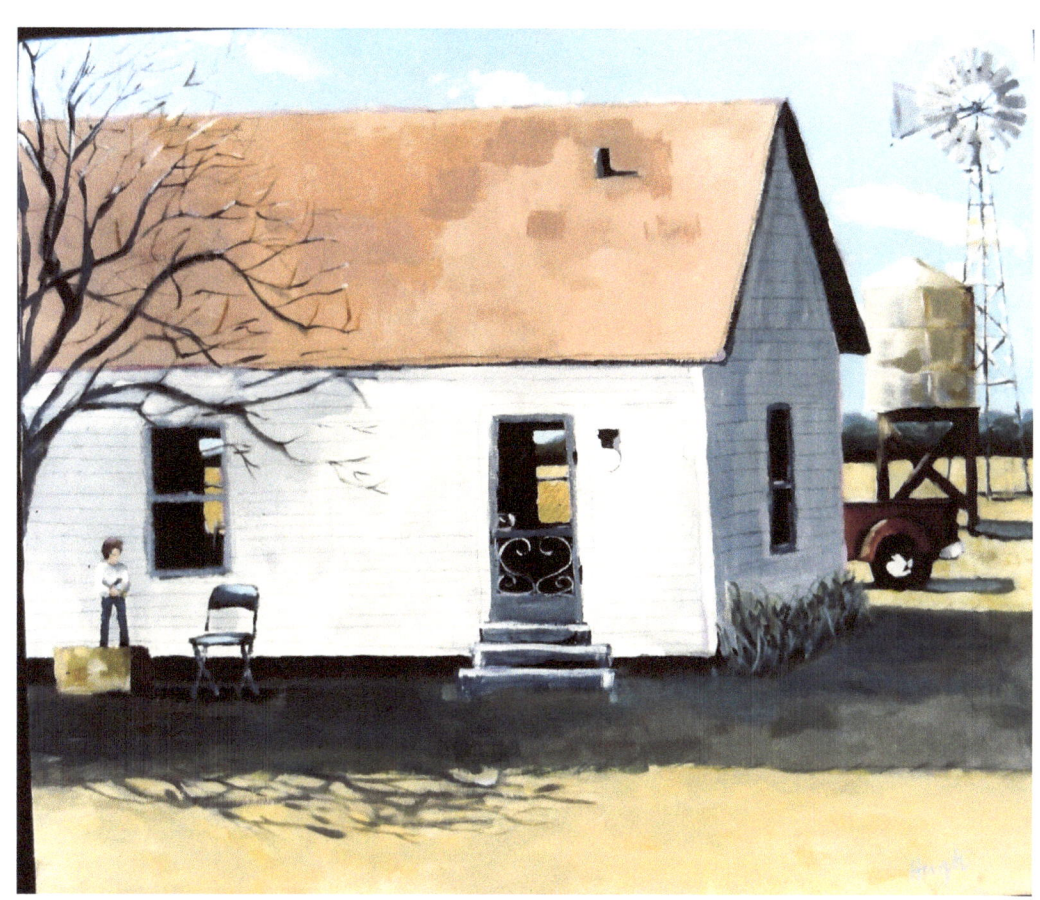

Sunday Afternoon, circa 1975, acrylic on canvas

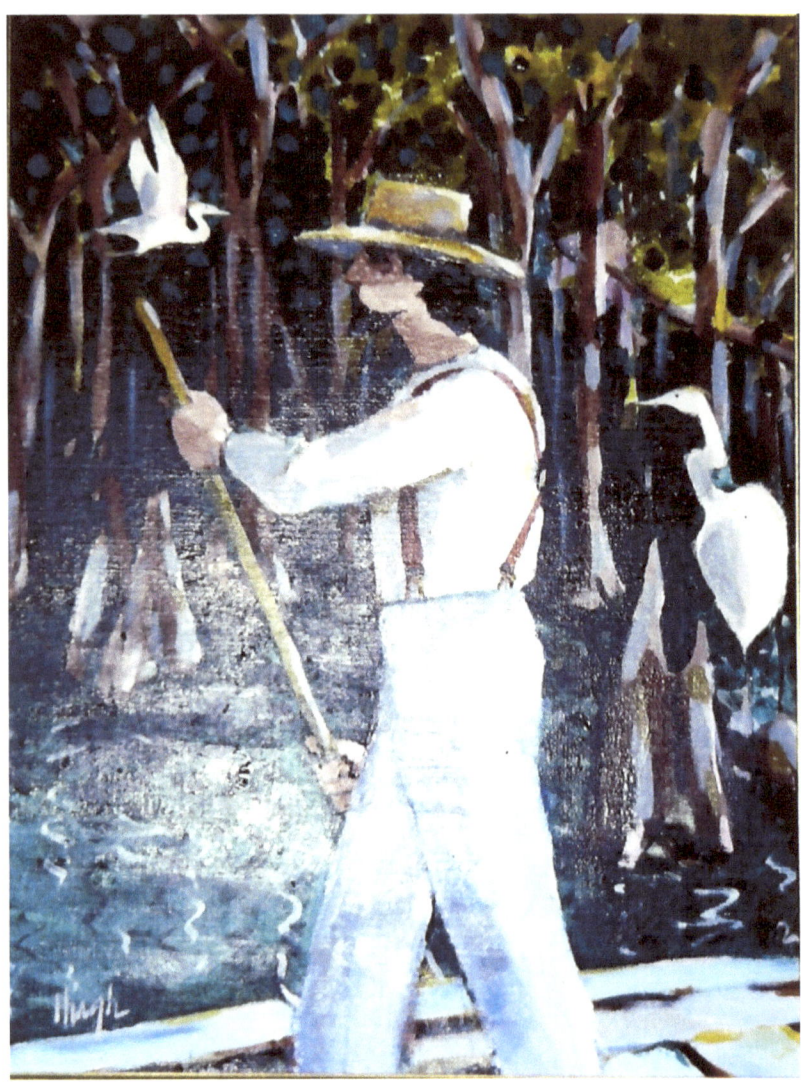

On the Bayou, circa 1989, acrylic on canvas

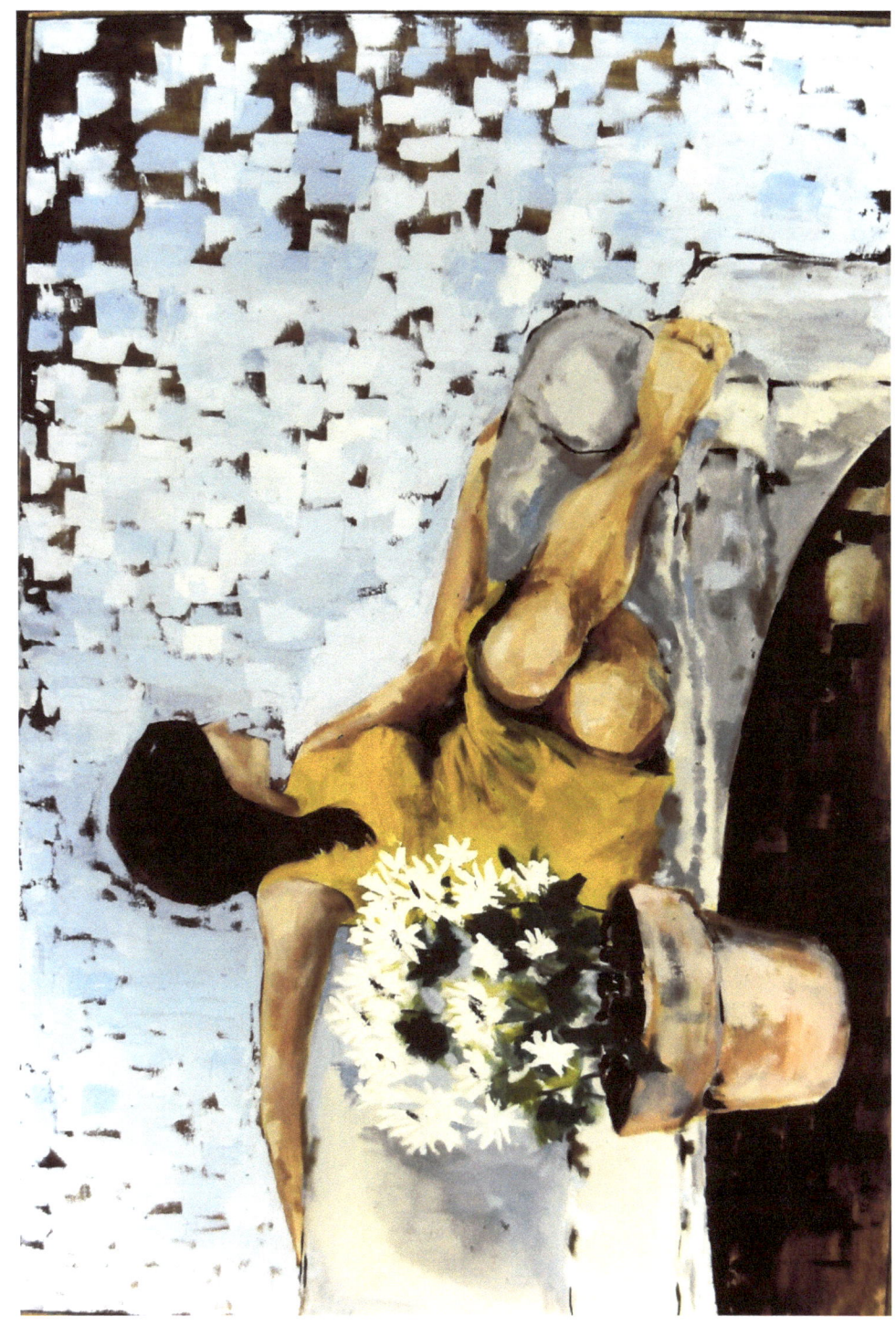

Woman on Sofa, circa 1965, oil on canvas

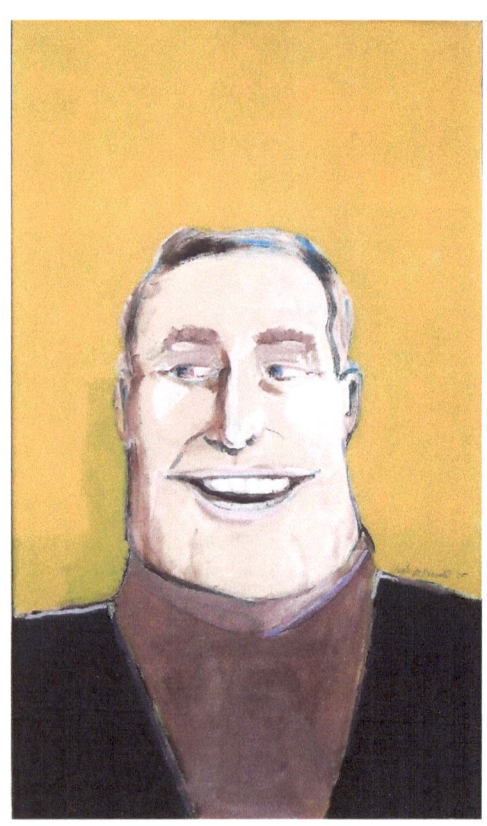

Meeter & Greeter, 2005, acrylic on canvas

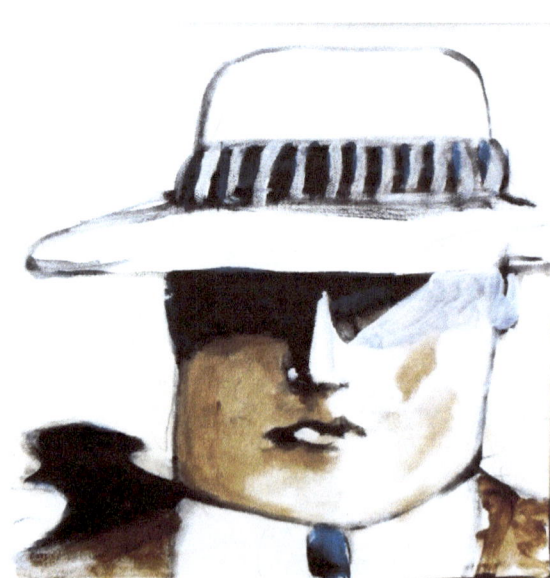

The Boxhead Don, 1990, acrylic & pencil

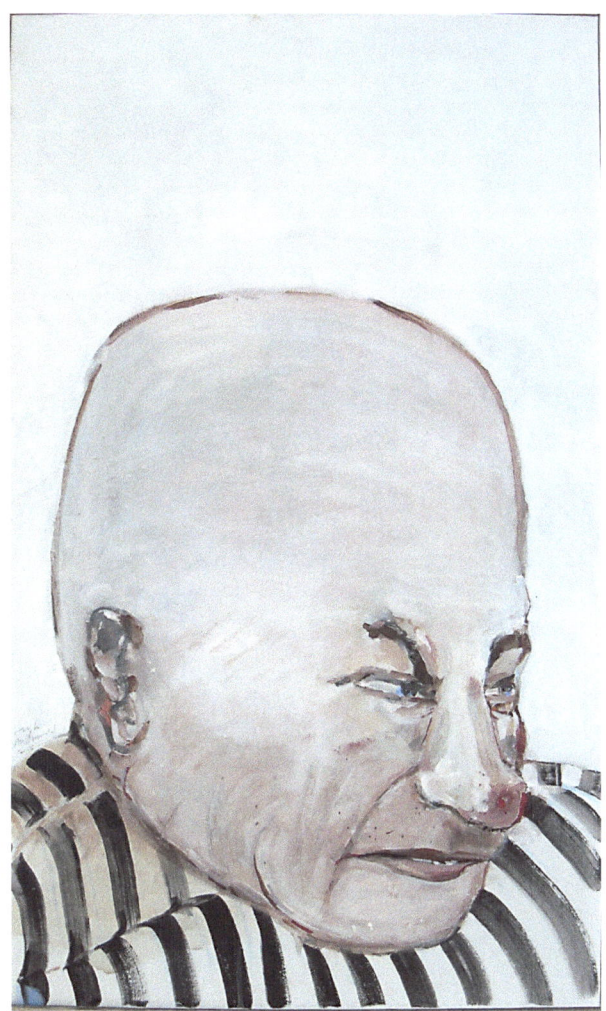

Black-and-White Collar Criminal, 2005, acrylic on canvas

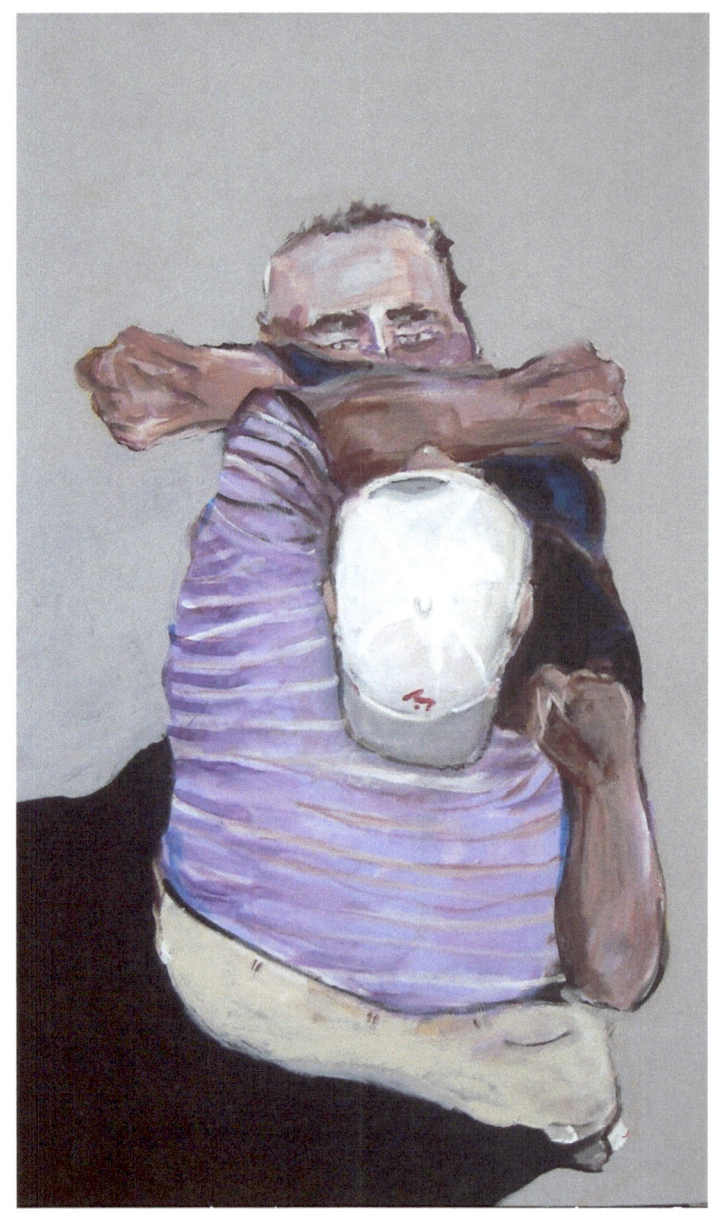

Fight, 2005, acrylic on canvas

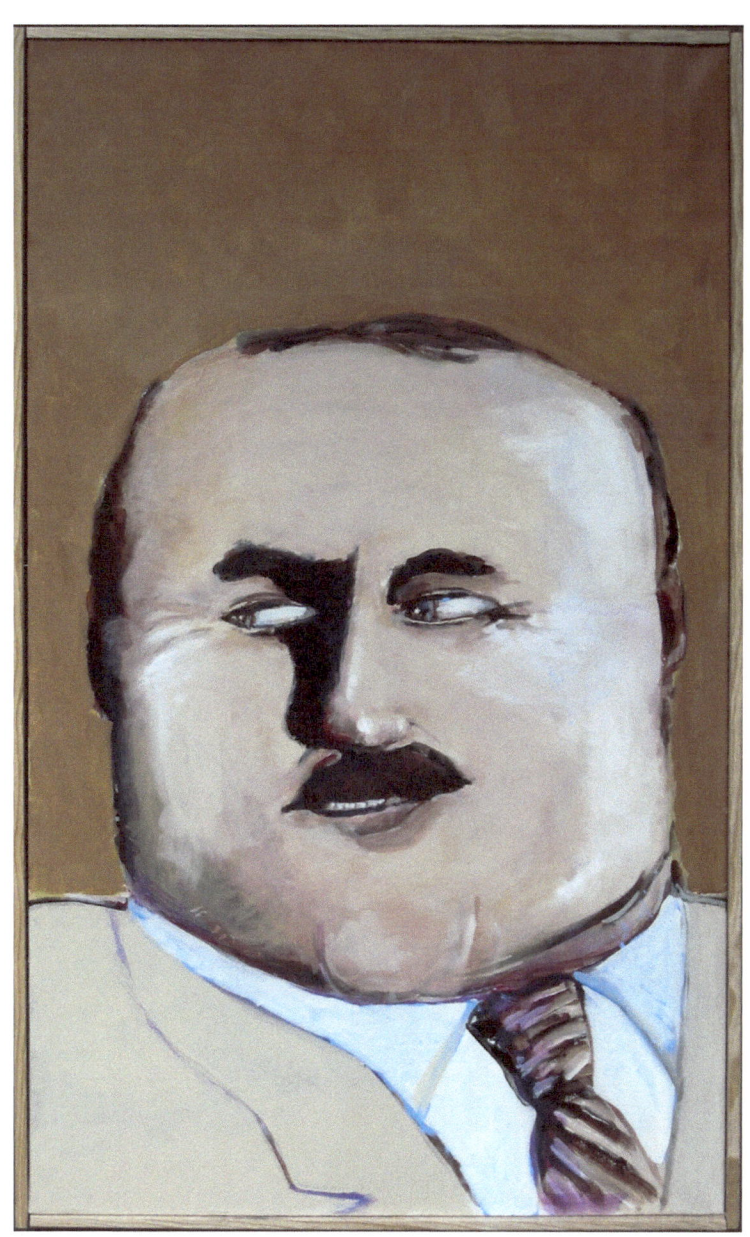

Kerouac's Publisher, 2005, acrylic on canvas

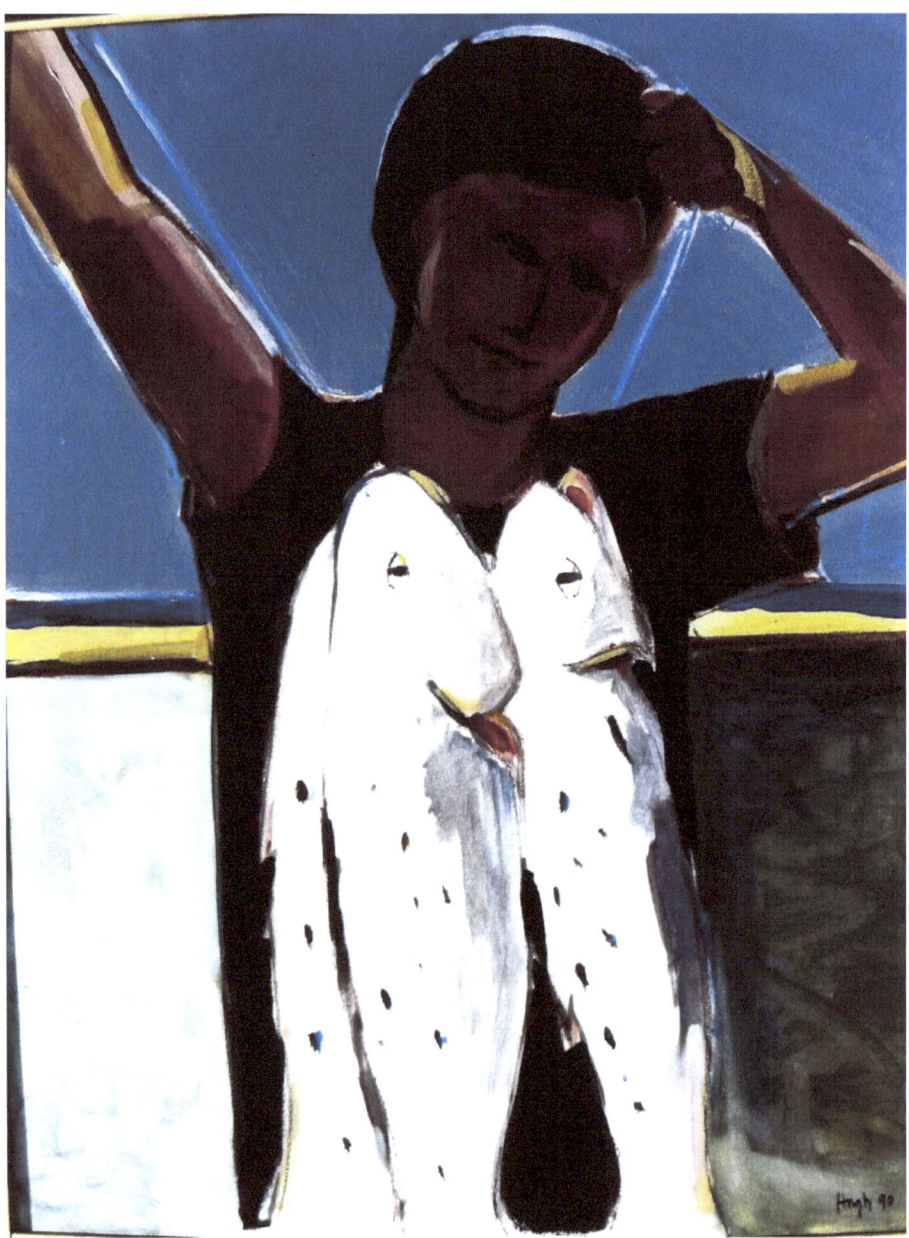

The Catch, 1990, acrylic on canvas

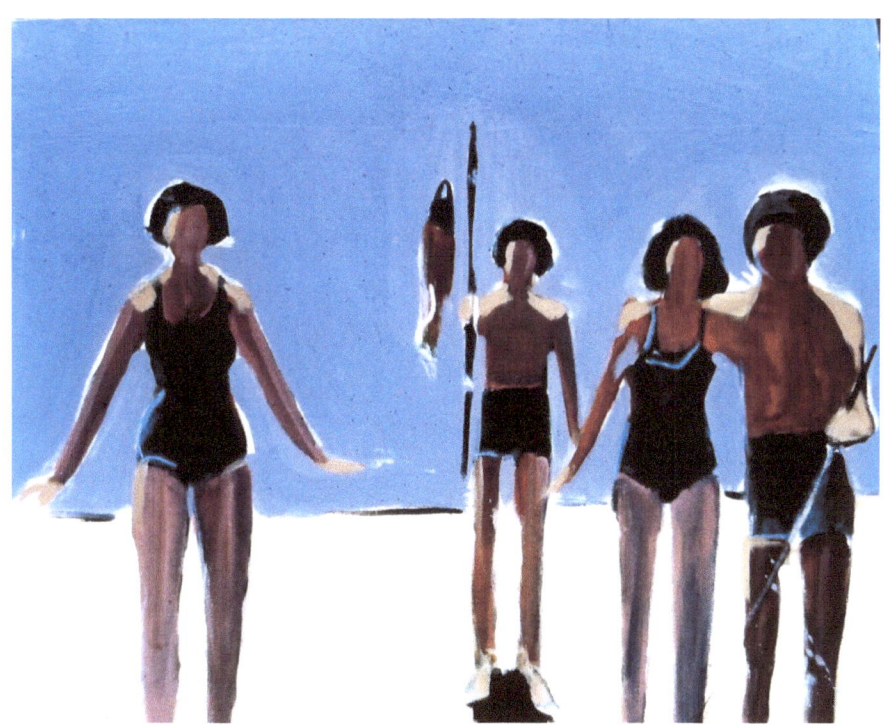

Beach Day, circa 1983, acrylic on canvas

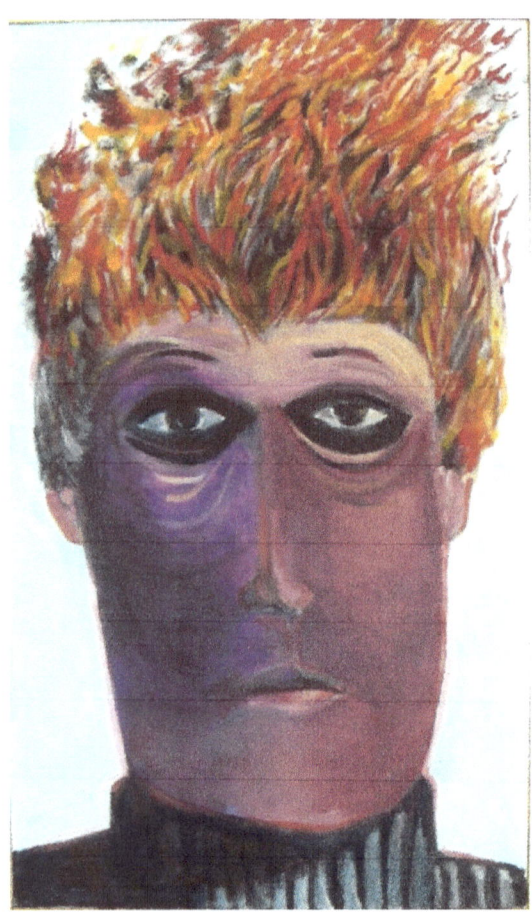

Pelo del Fuego, 2005, acrylic on canvas

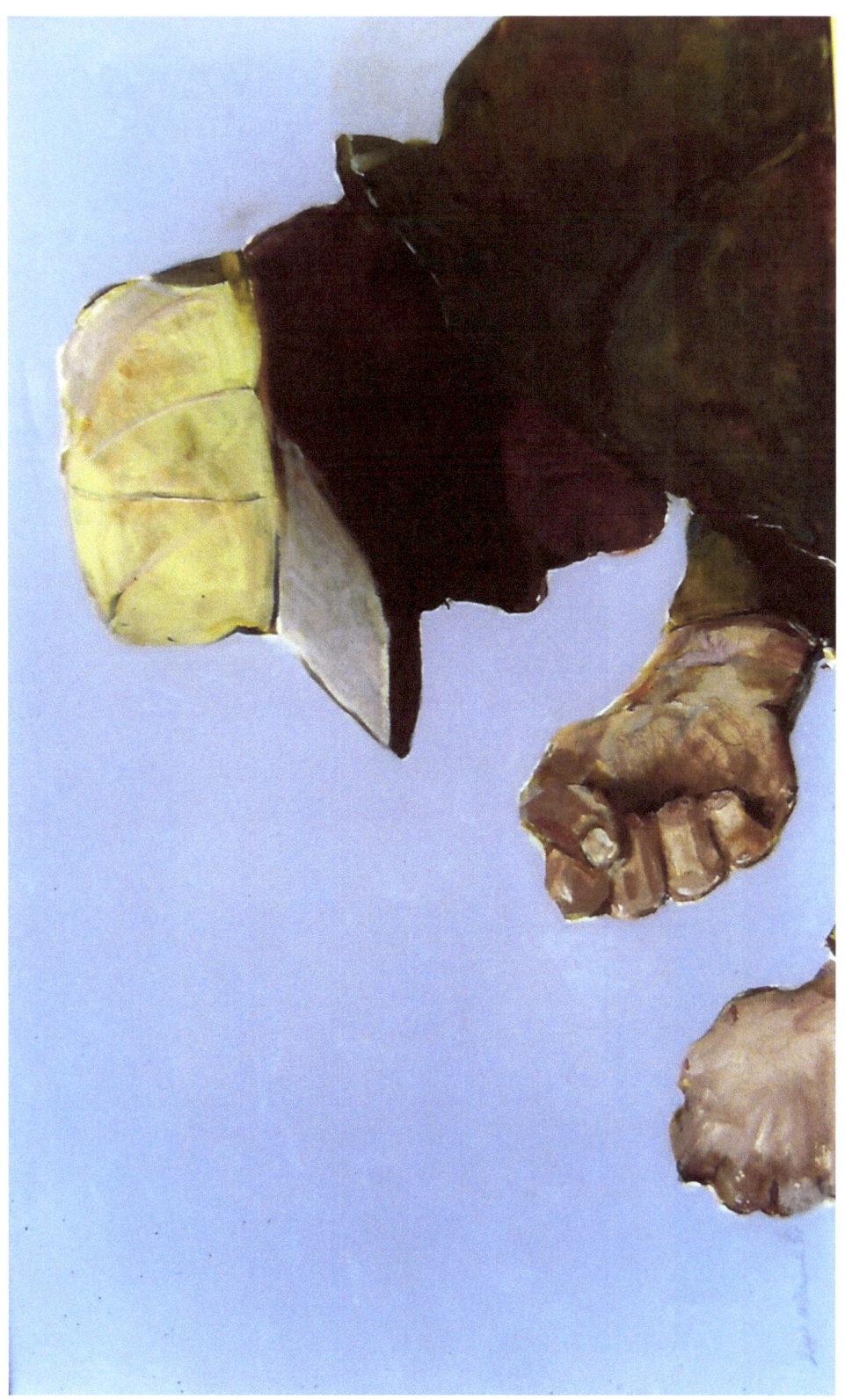

Hardway, 2006, acrylic on canvas

3. places, nature…

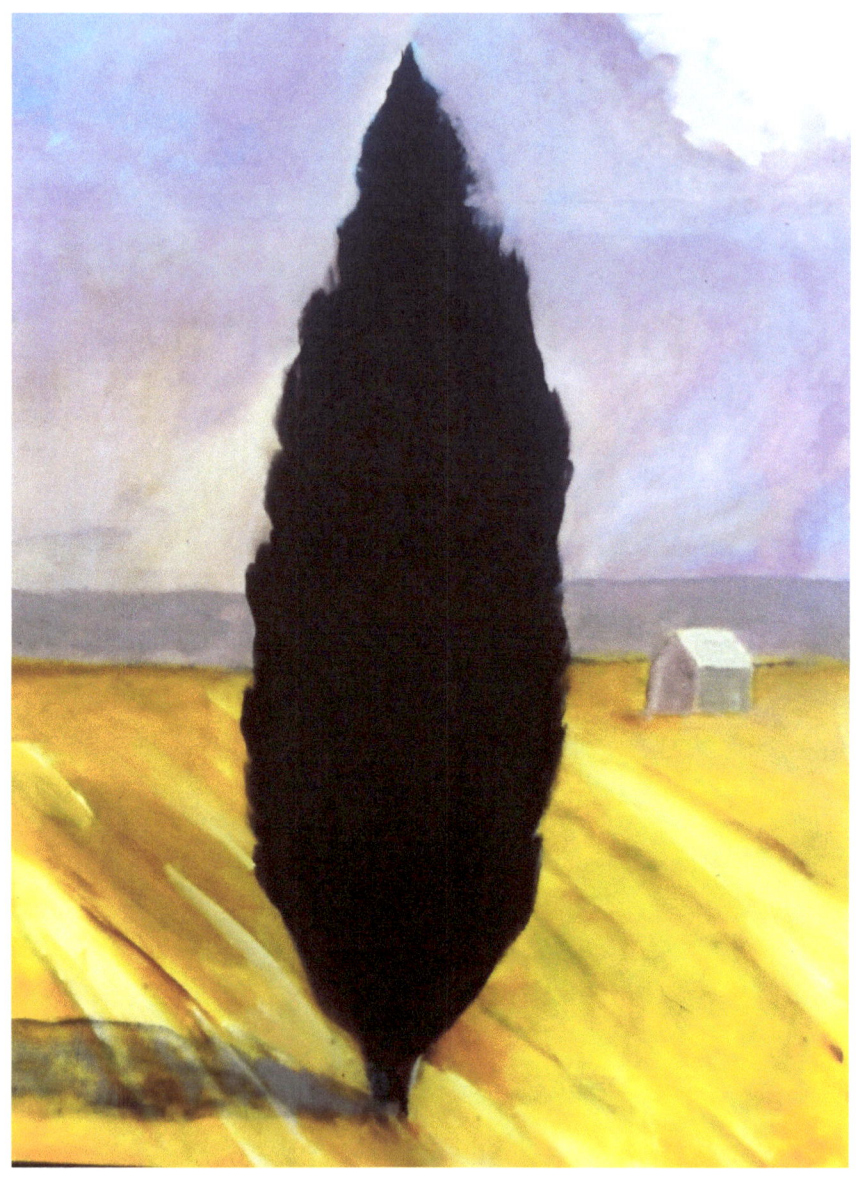

Northwest Cedar, 2000-2005, acrylic on canvas

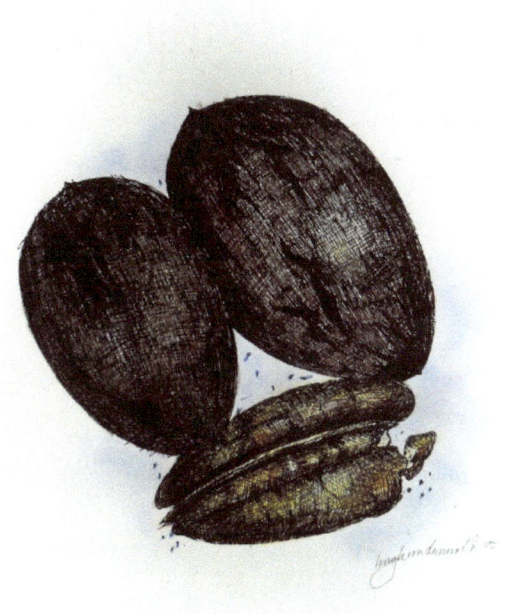

Pecans, 2000, ink and colored pencil

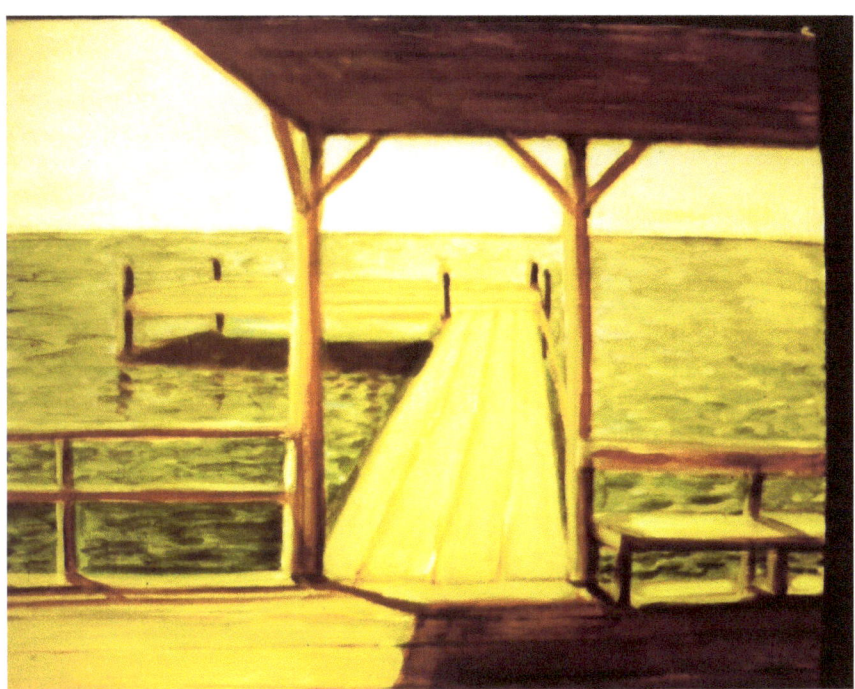

Pier, 1989, acrylic on canvas

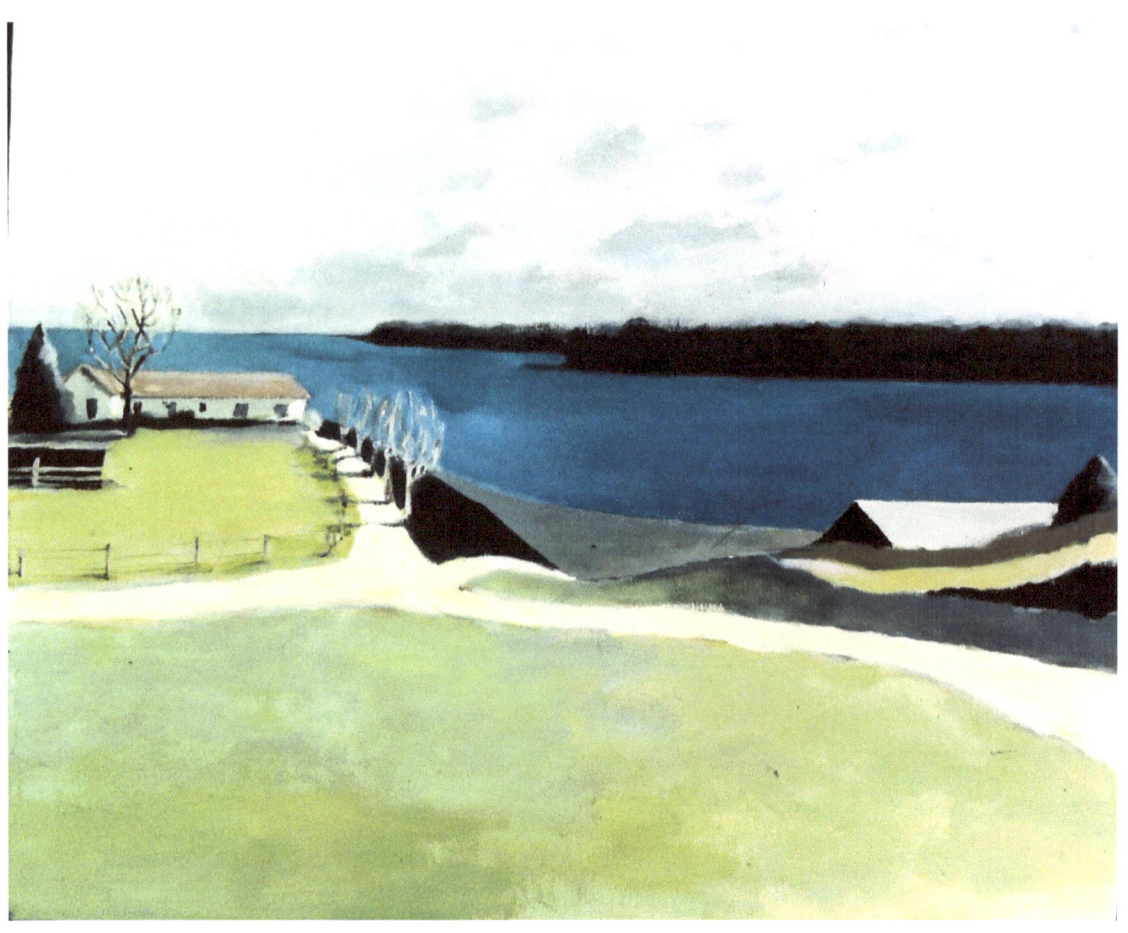

The View from There, circa 1999, acrylic on canvas

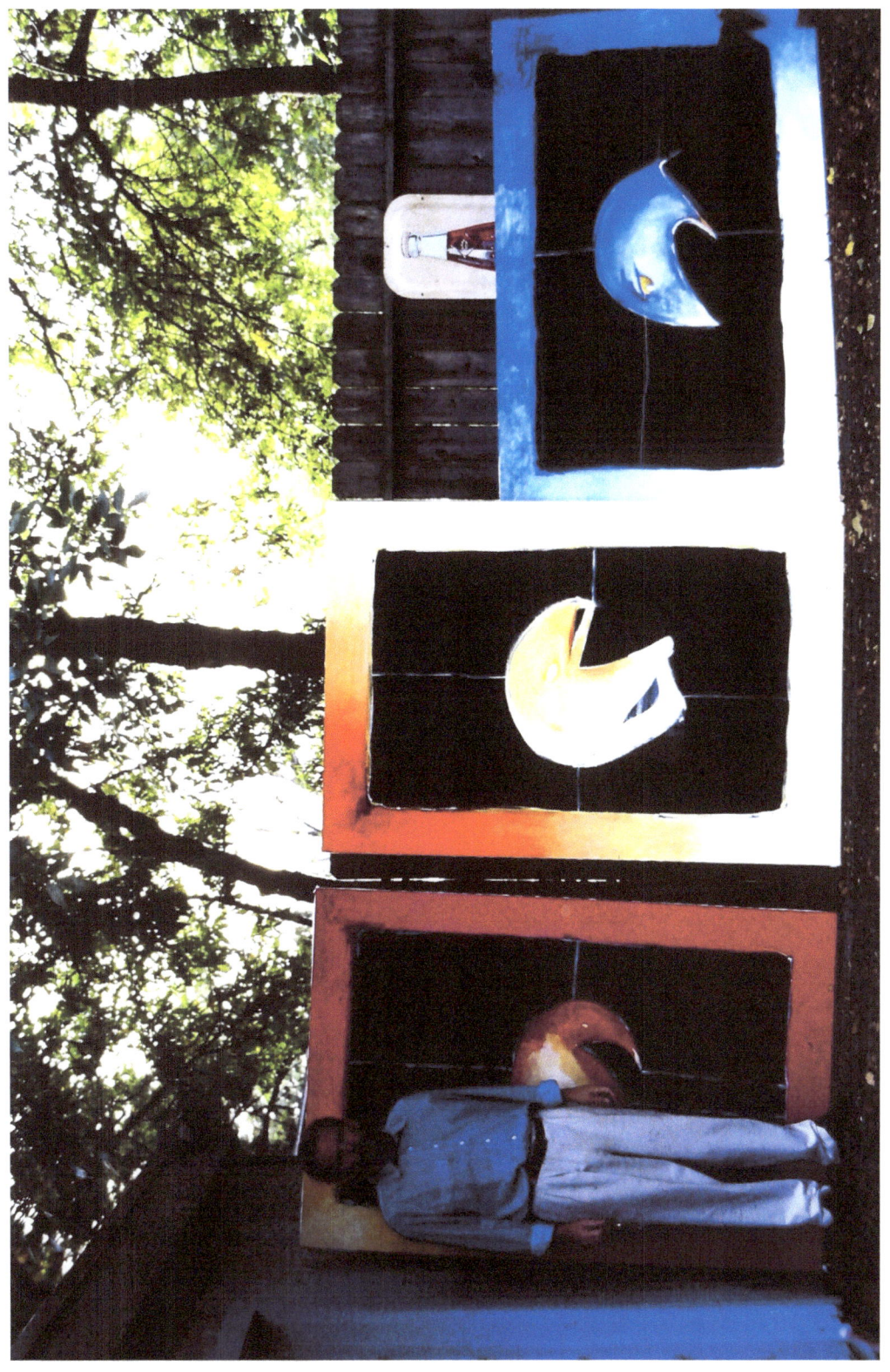

Bird Head Trio (with artist), 1991, acrylic on canvas

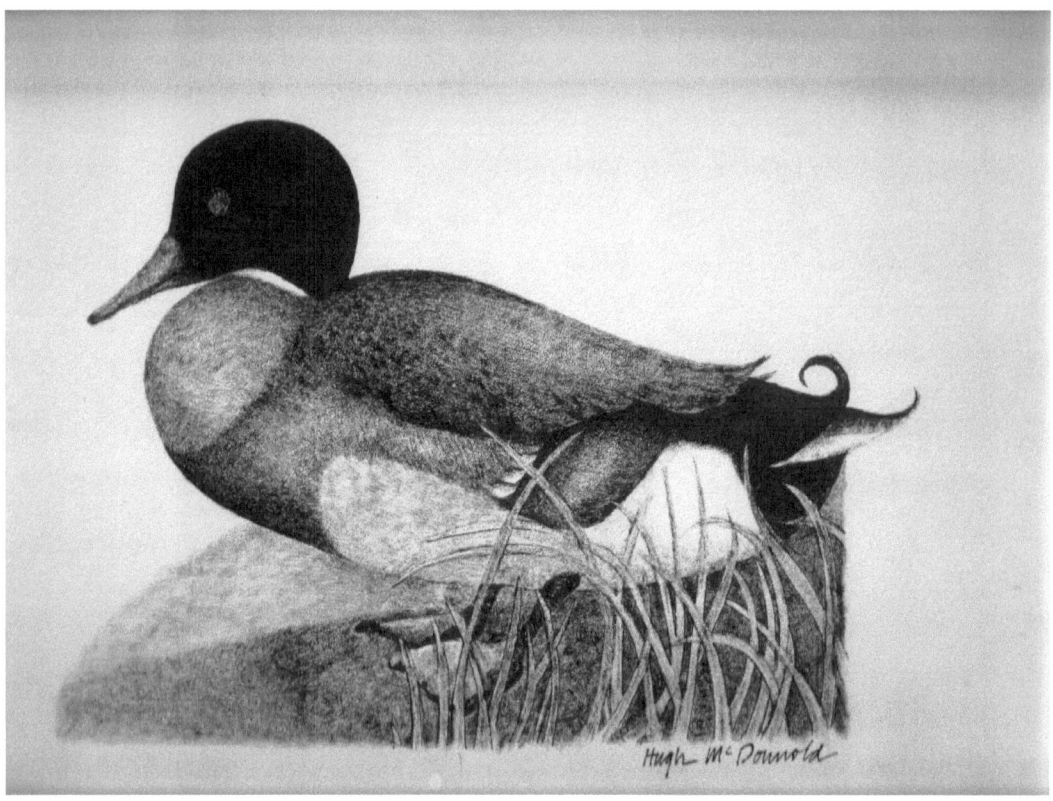

Mallard, circa 1972, ink on paper

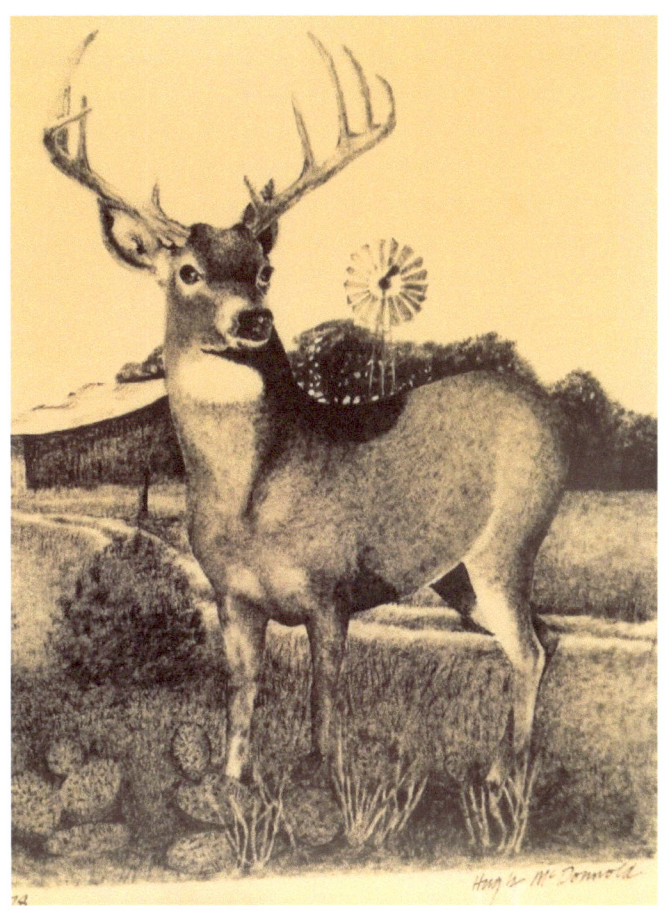

Hill Country *Buck*, circa 1972, ink on paper

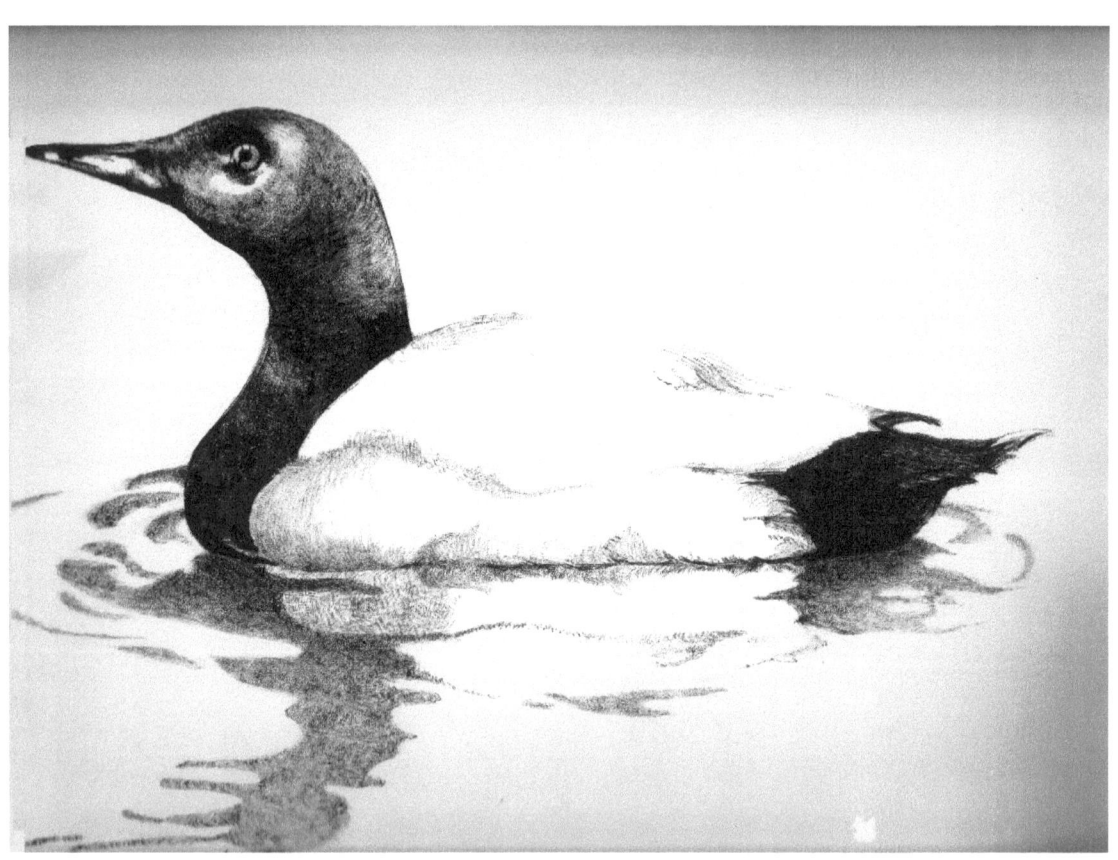

Duck on Water, circa 1972, ink on paper

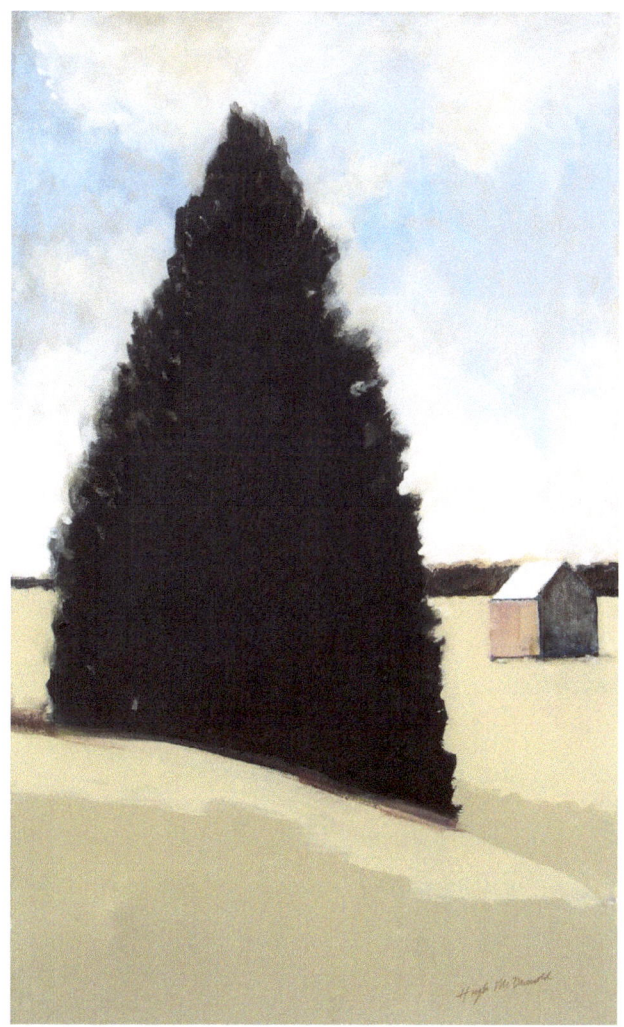

Texas Cedar, 2000-2005, oil on canvas

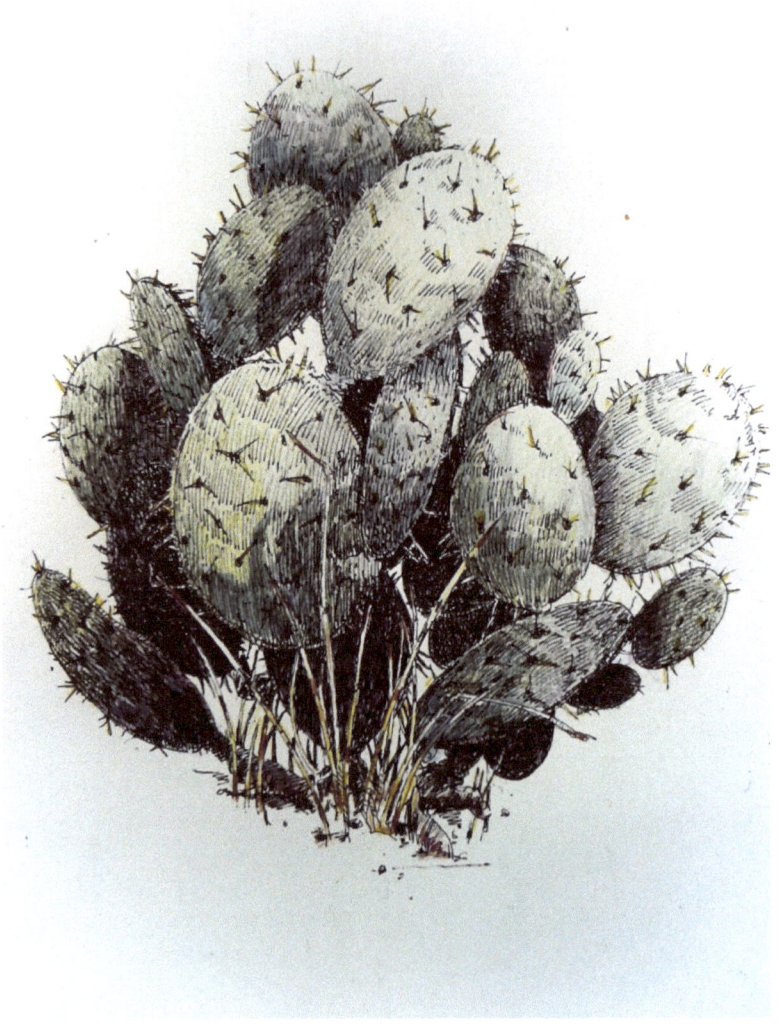

Prickly Pear Cactus, 2000, ink and colored pencil

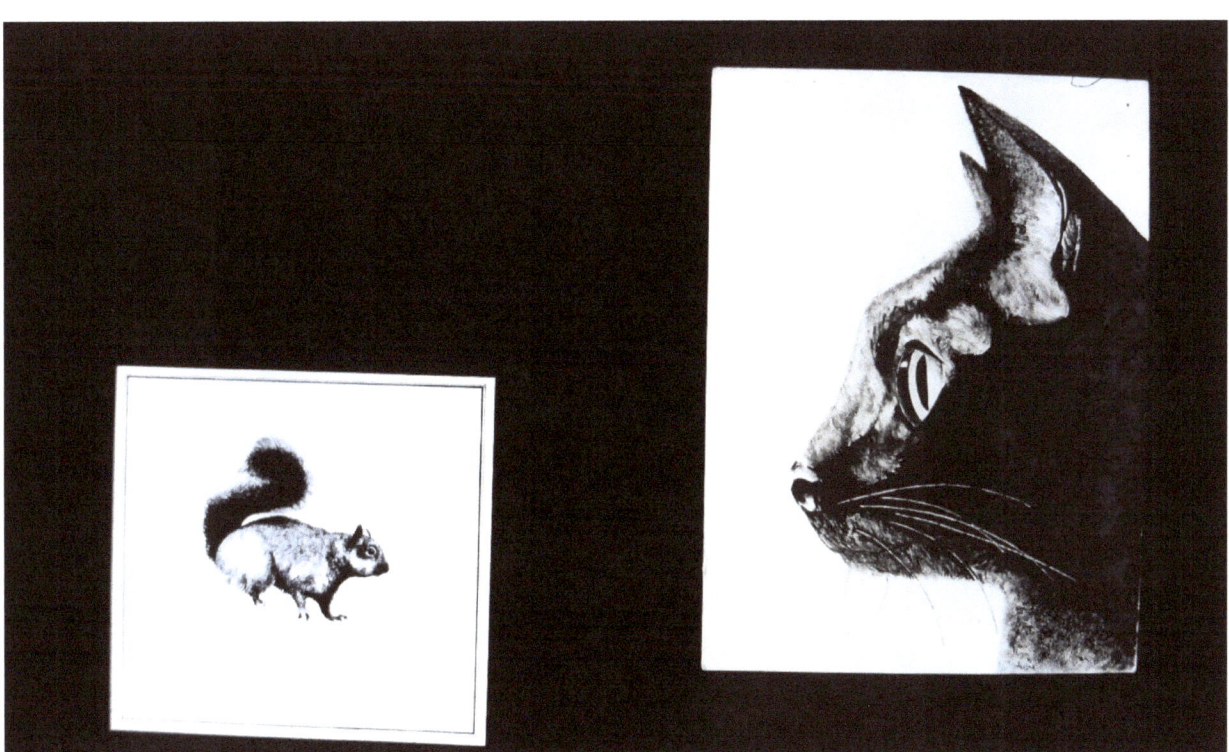

Cat and Squirrel, 1995-2000, ink on paper

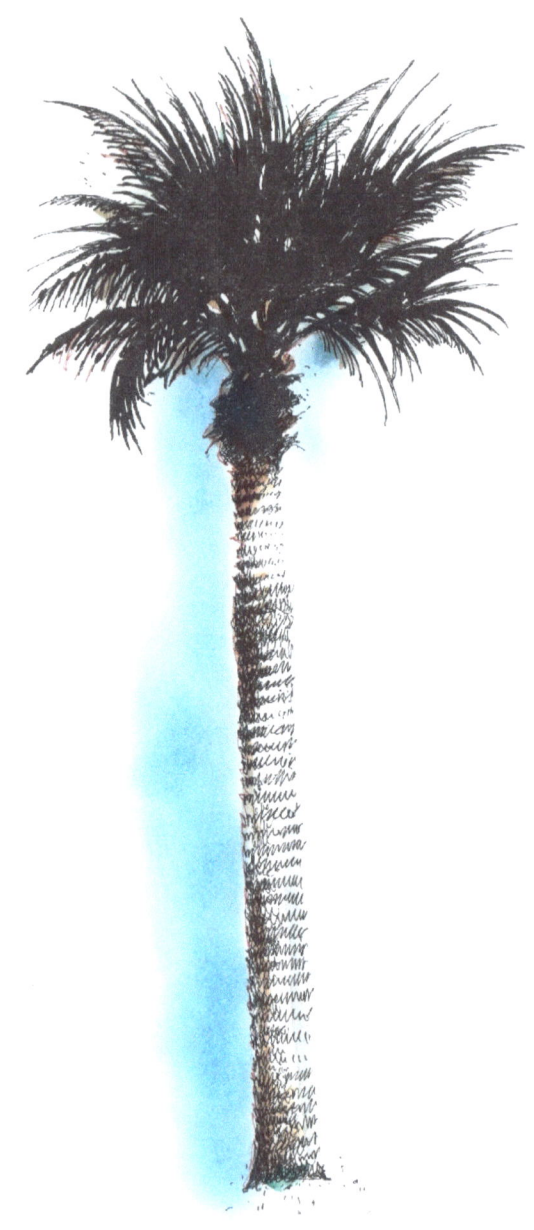

Rockport Palm, 2000, ink and colored pencil

4. abstracts

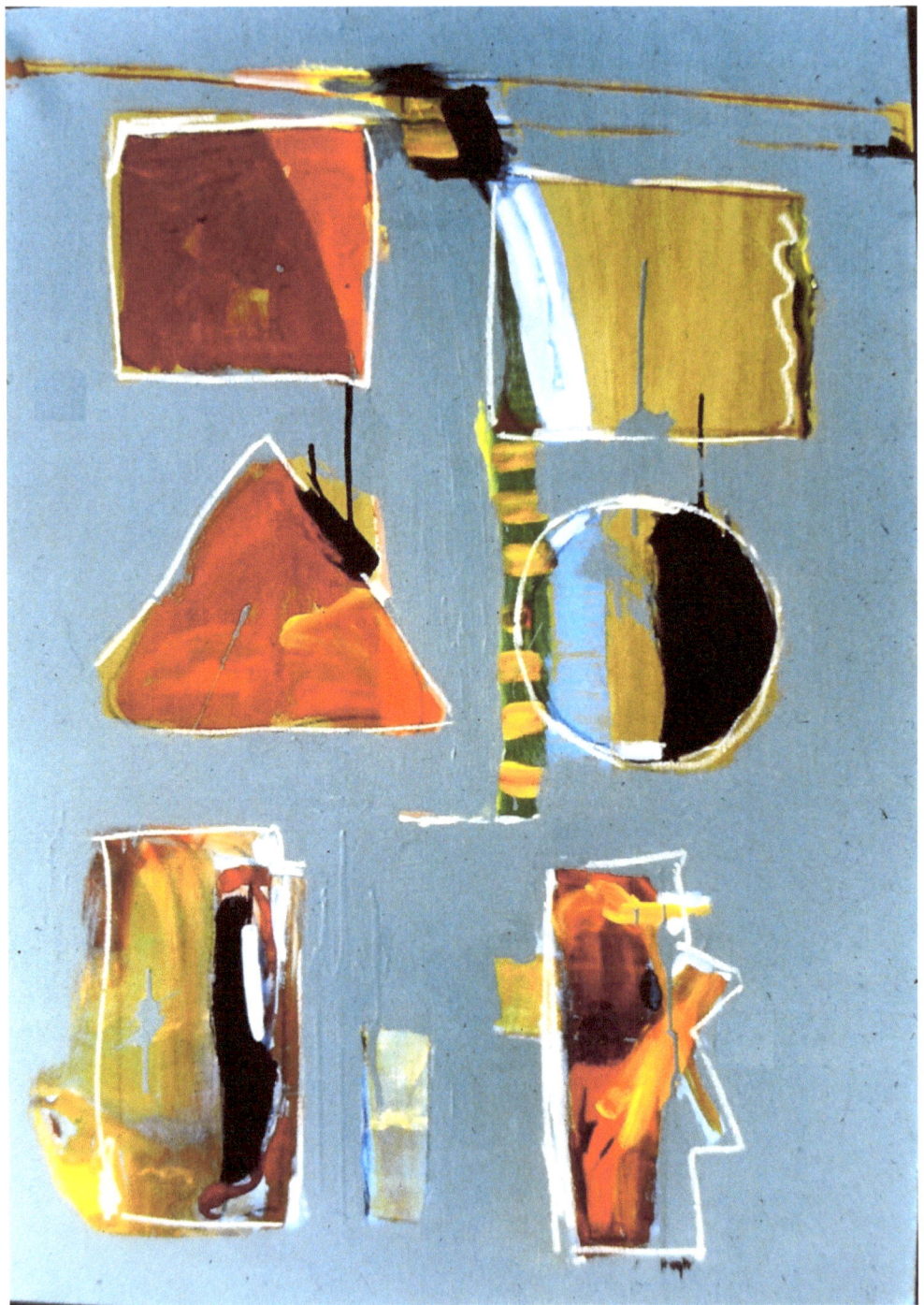

Totem, circa 1990, acrylic/oil on canvas

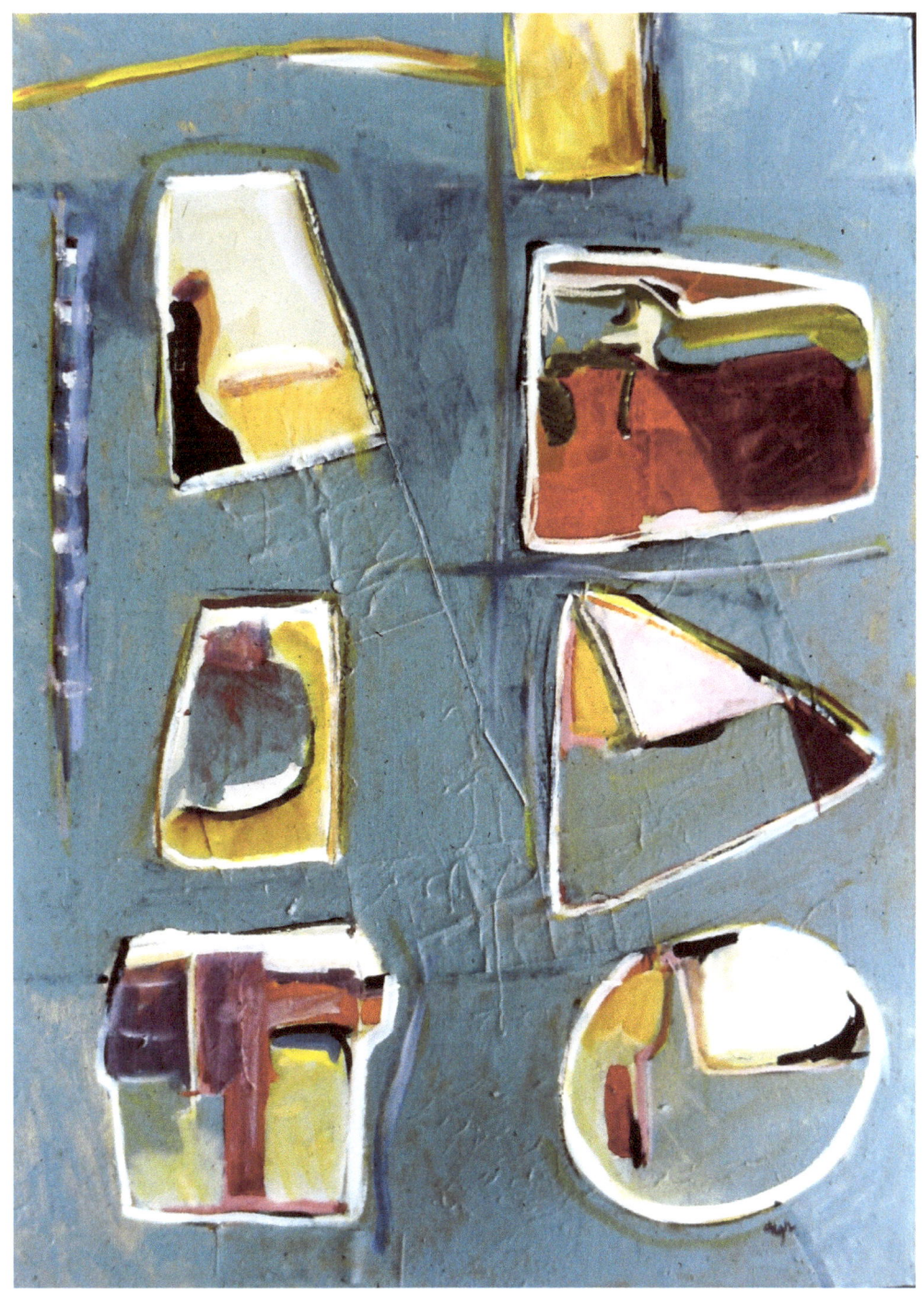

Totem 2, circa 1990, acrylic/oil on canvas

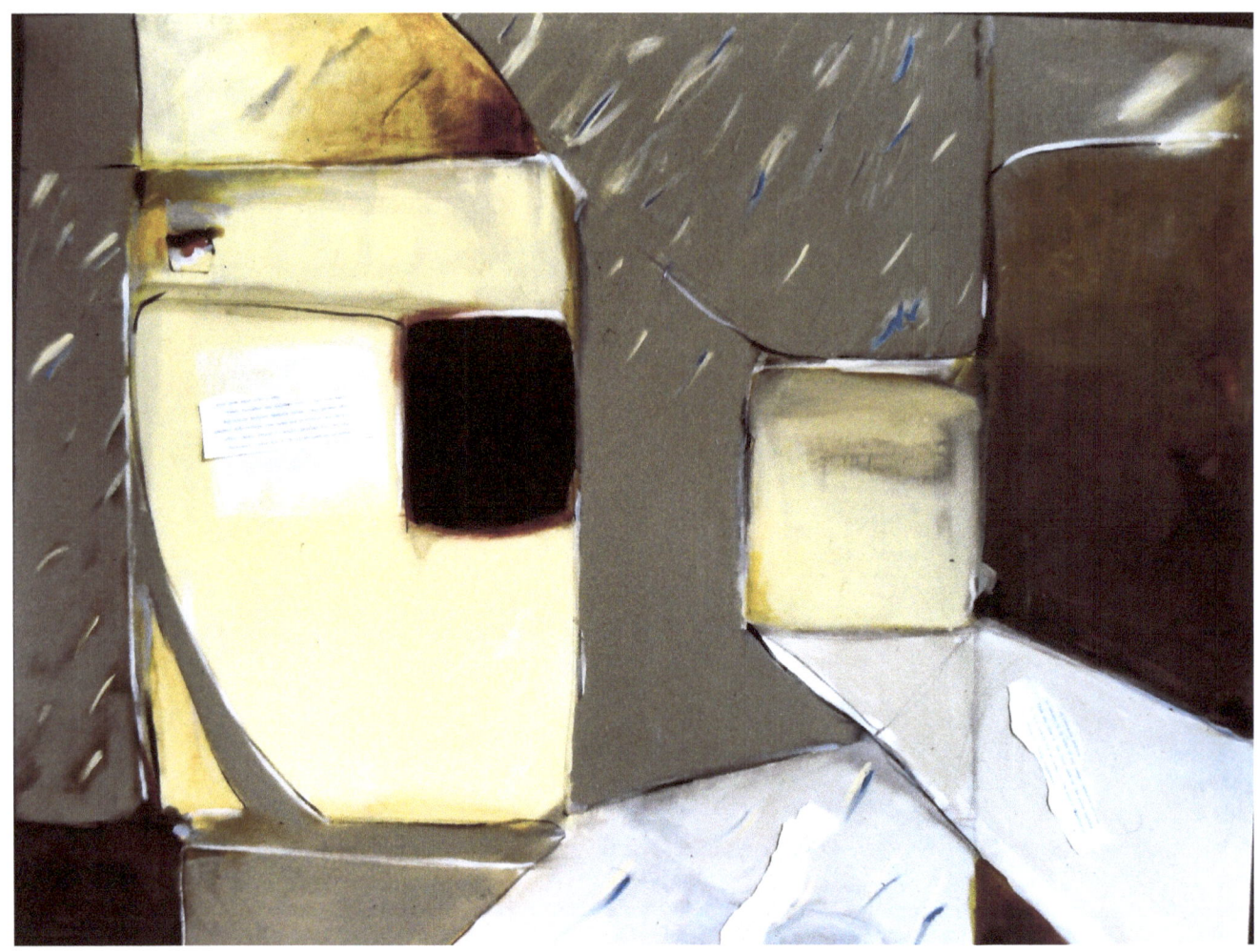

Box Heart, 1991, mixed media

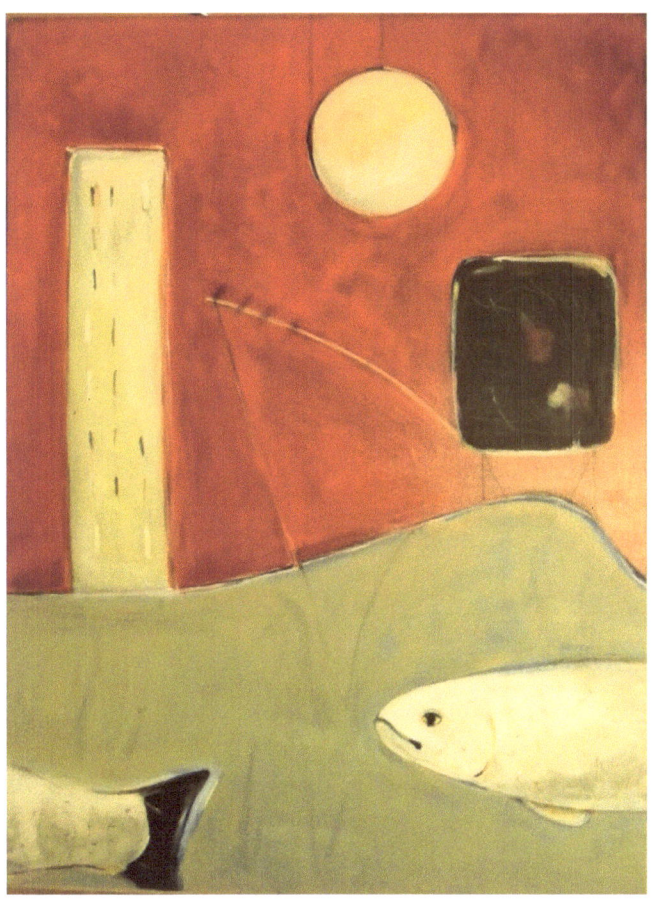

Spawning Season, 1985-1990, acrylic on canvas

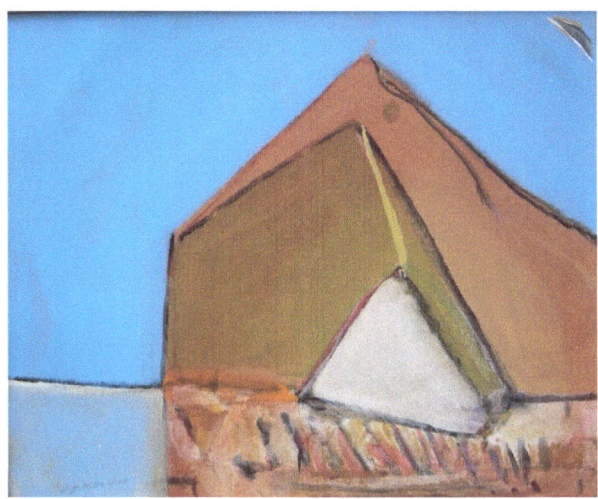

Tent Camp, date unknown, oil on canvas

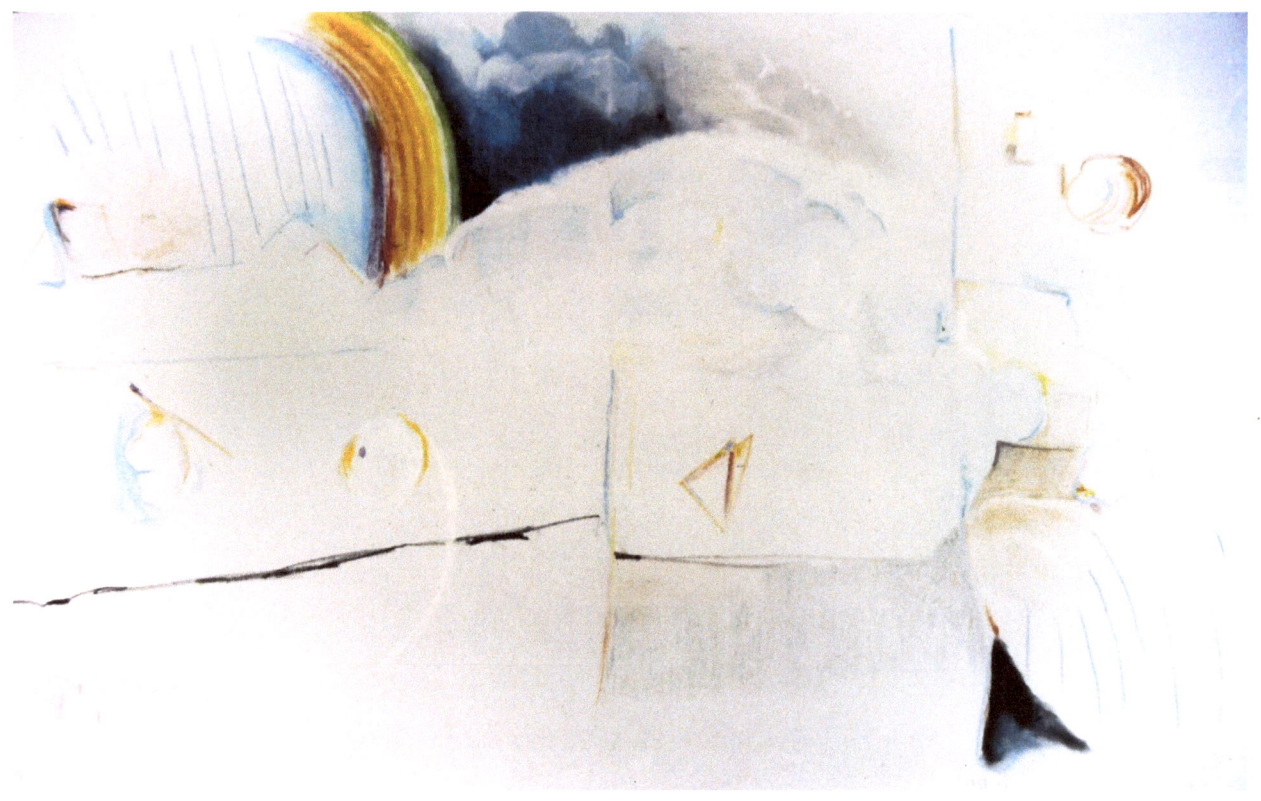

Sky from the Backseat of a '57 Chevy, 1985, oil and pastel

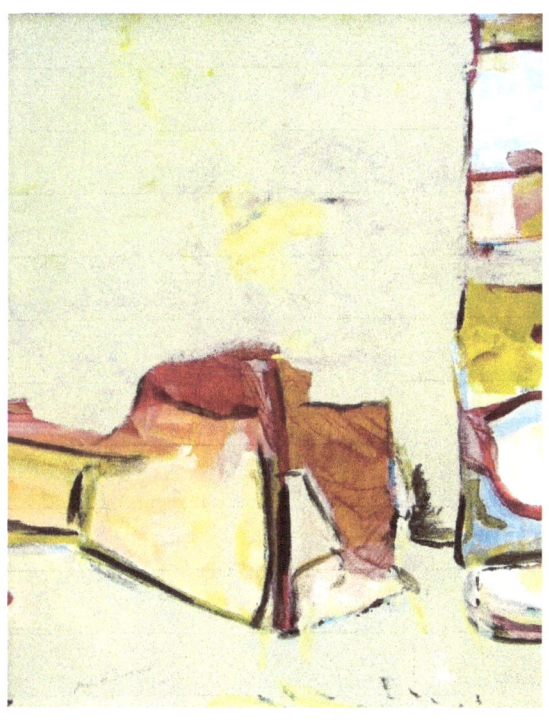

Auto House, 1998-2003, oil on canvas

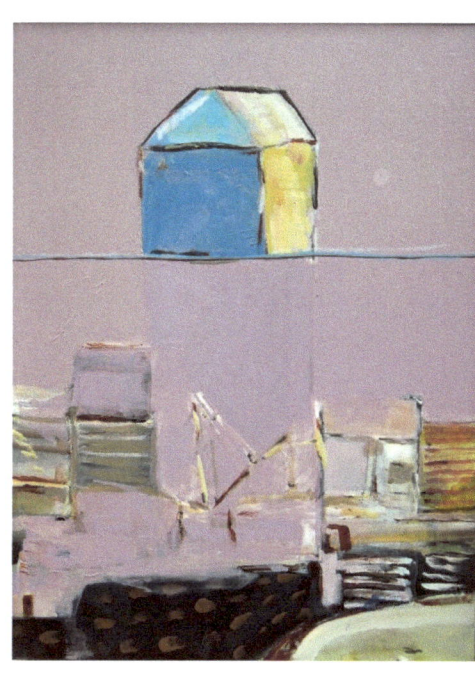

Pier and Beam, 2000-2005, oil on canvas

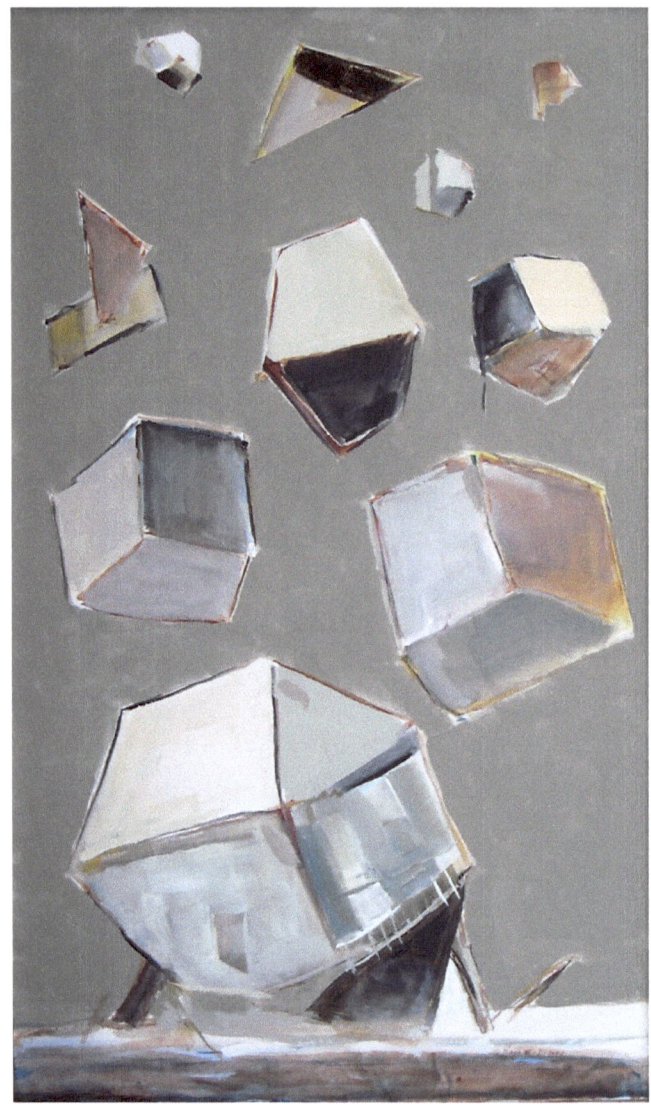

Real Estate Rising, 2005, acrylic on canvas

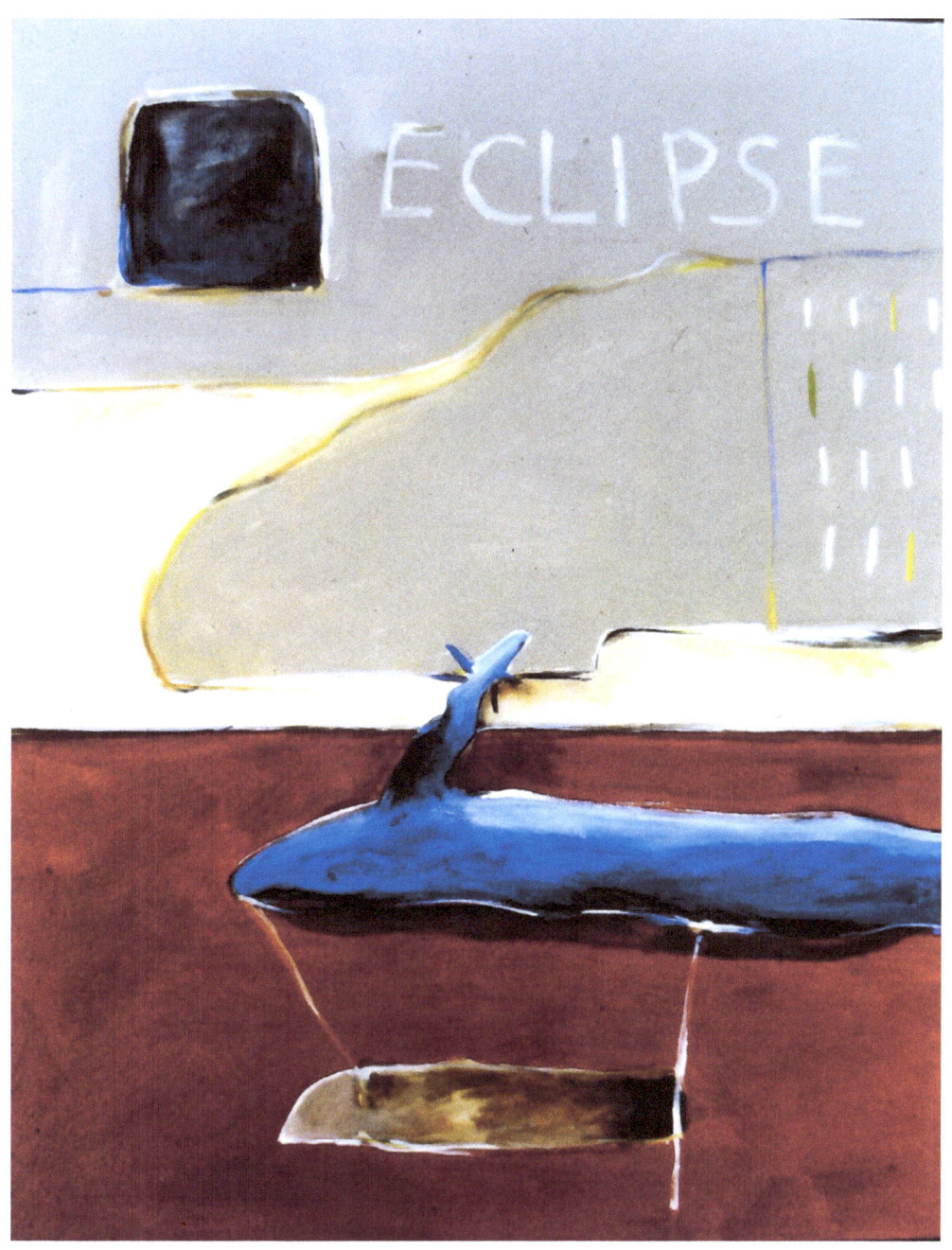

Eclipse, 1991, acrylic on canvas

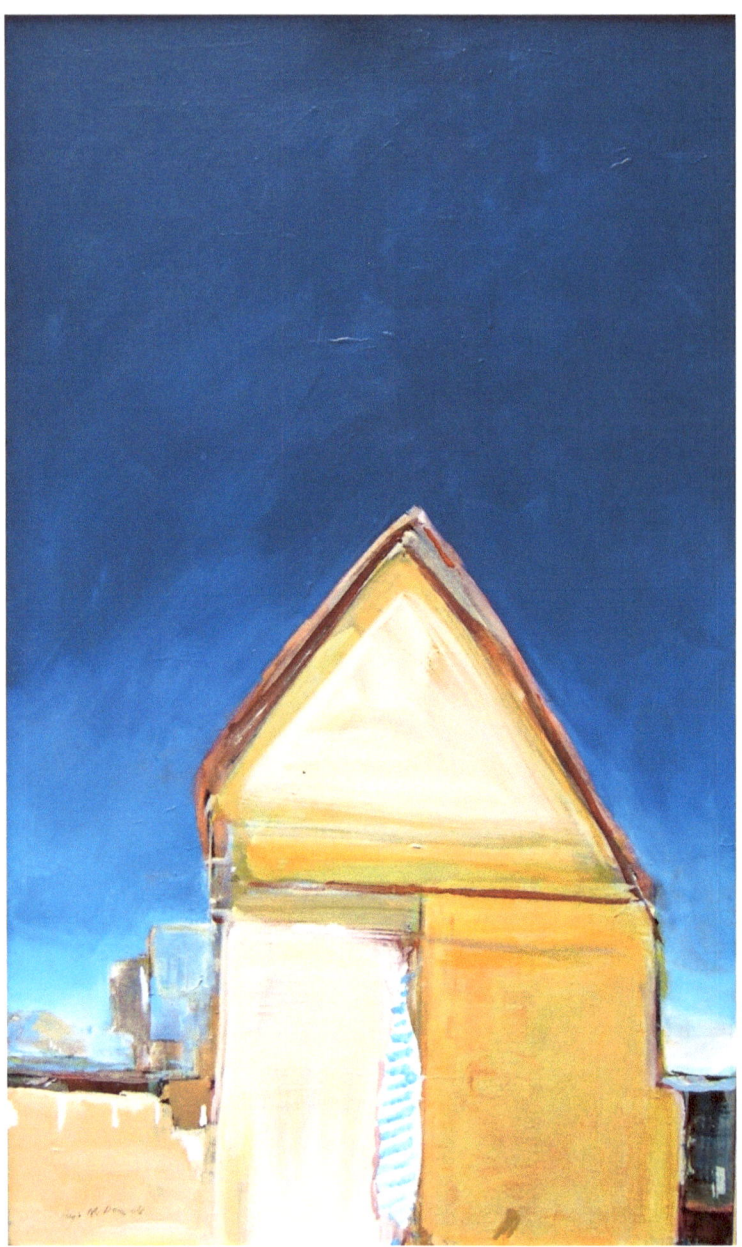

Fracture House, circa 2004, oil on canvas

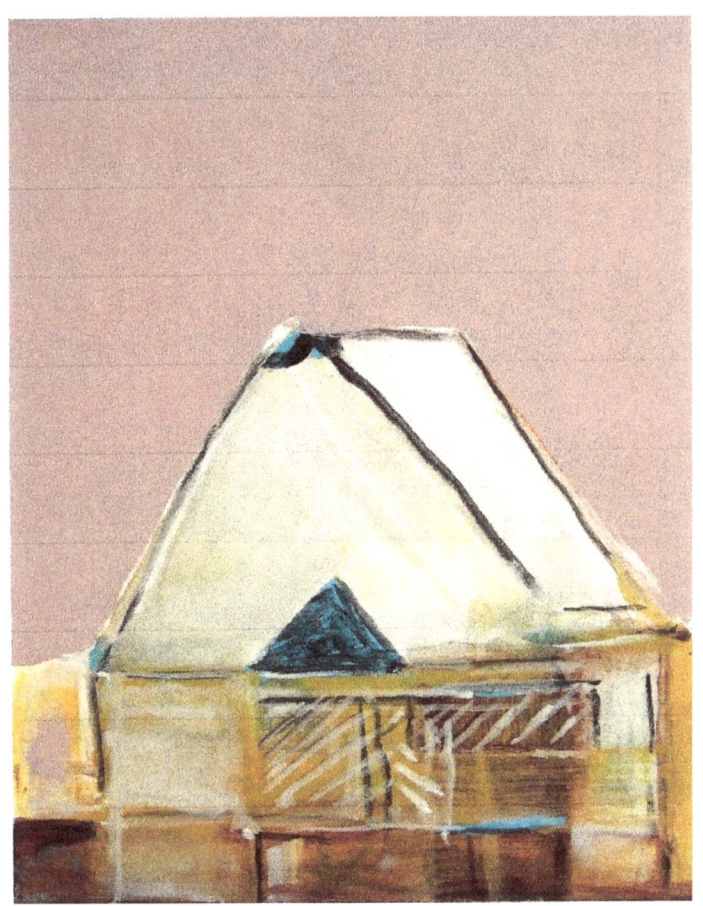

Gross Geometry, circa 2006, oil on canvas

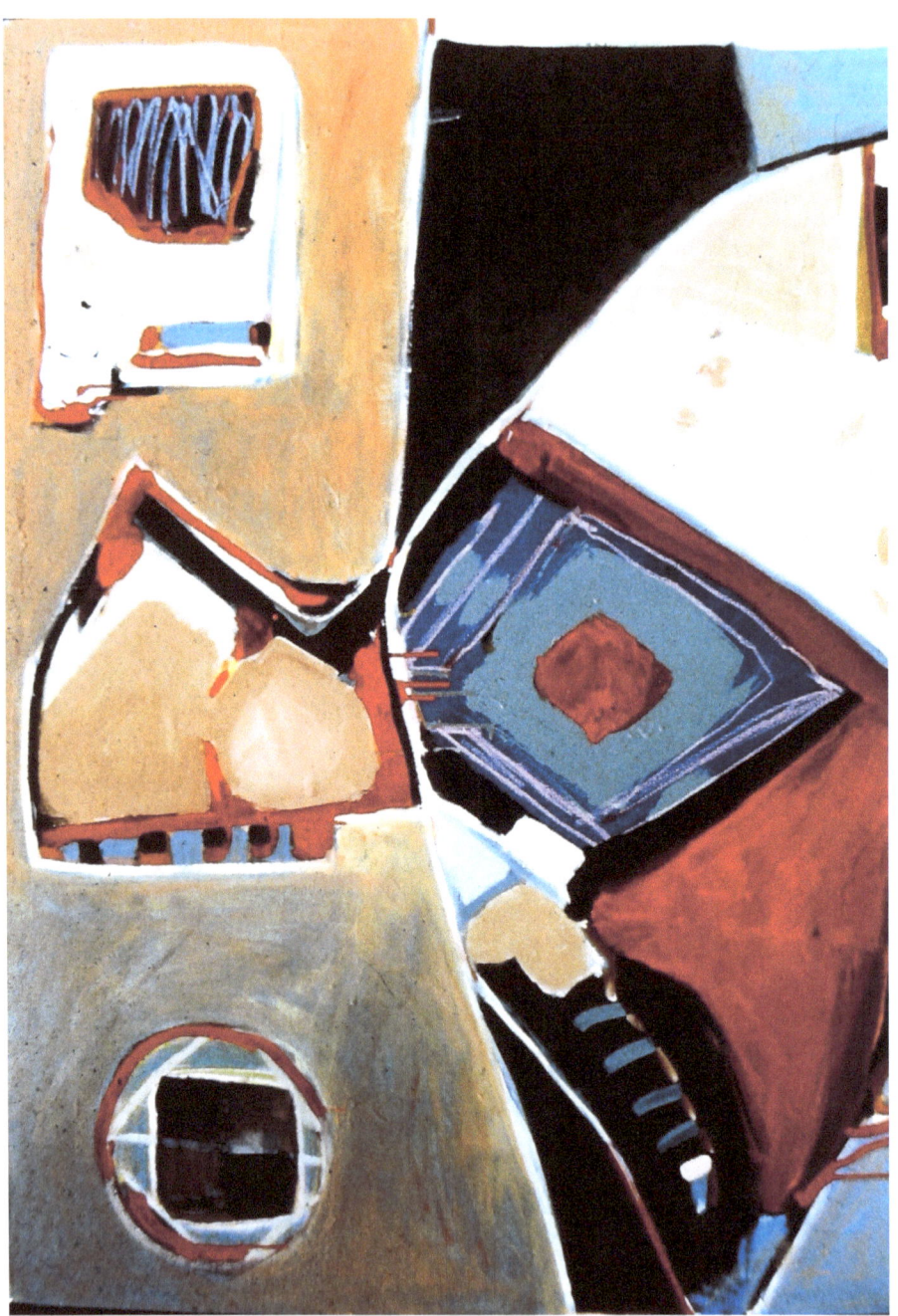

Rider, 1990, acrylic on canvas

5. misc.
(commercial art, sketches, sculpture, etc.)

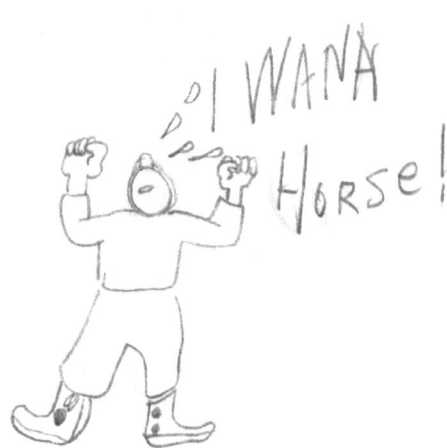

Early Drawing, 1945-1950

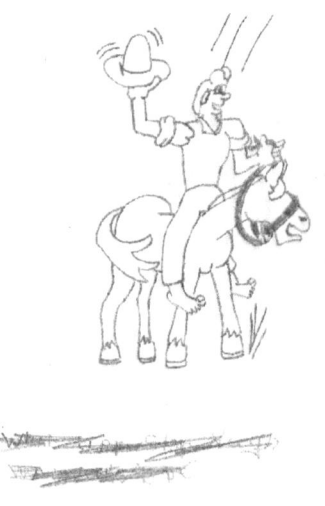

Early Drawing 1945-1950

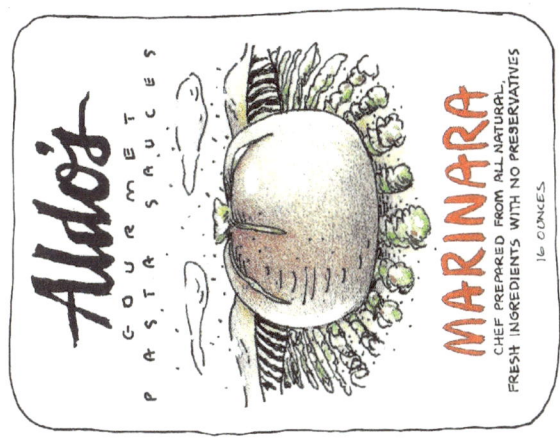

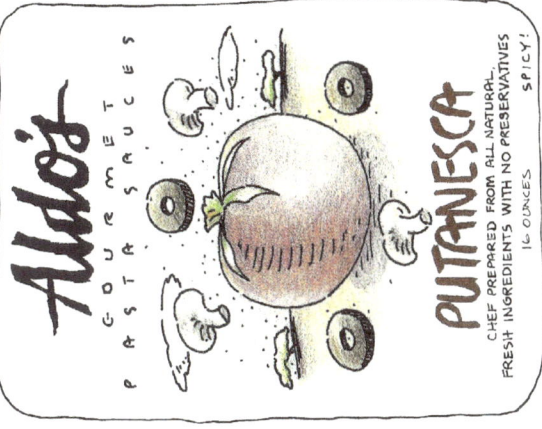

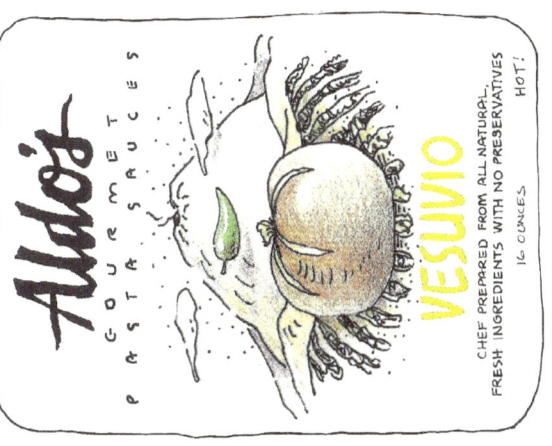

Pasta sauce labels, circa 1998

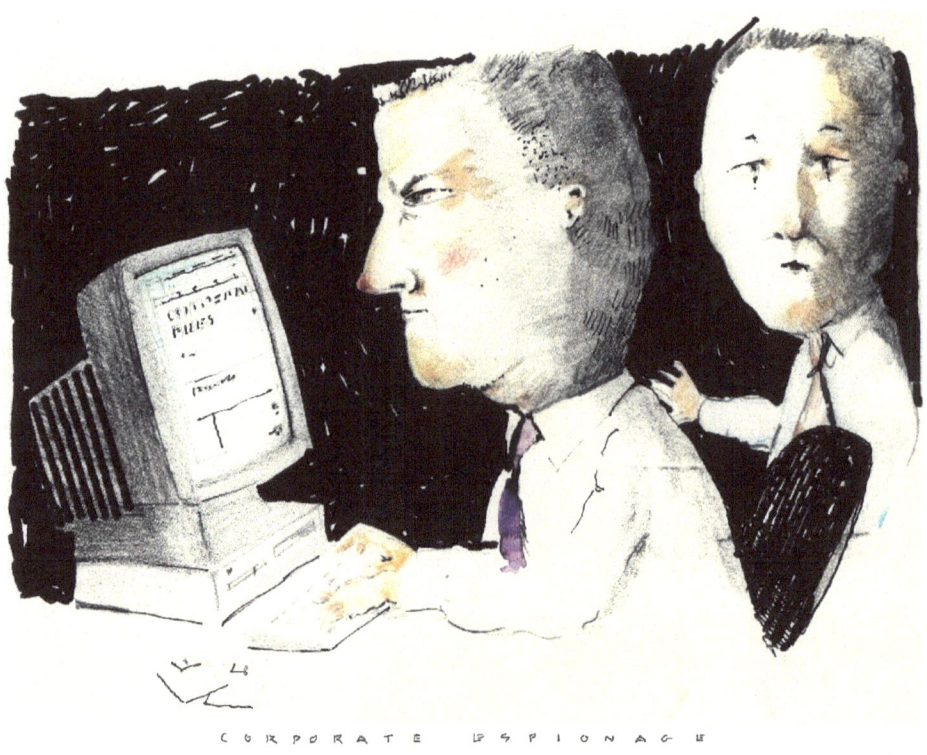

Drawing: *Corporate Espionage*, date unknown

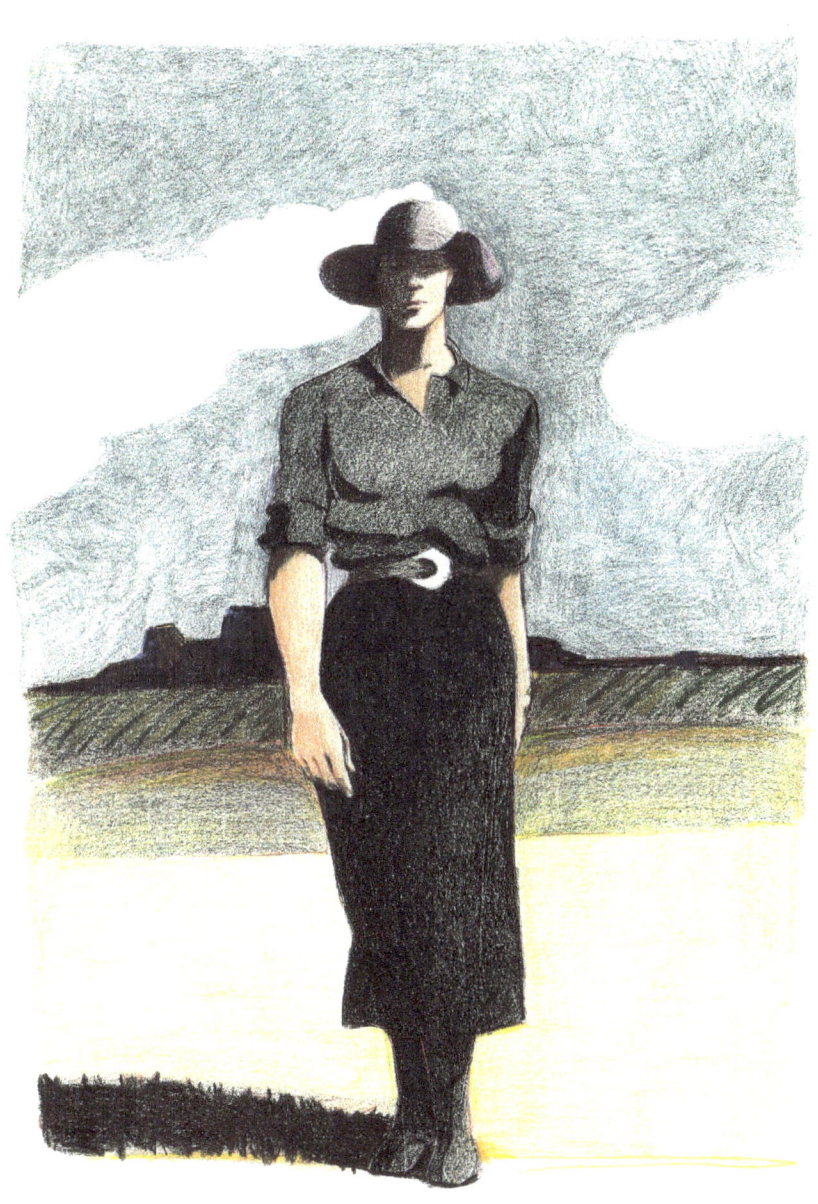

Plains Woman, circa 1989, colored pencil on paper

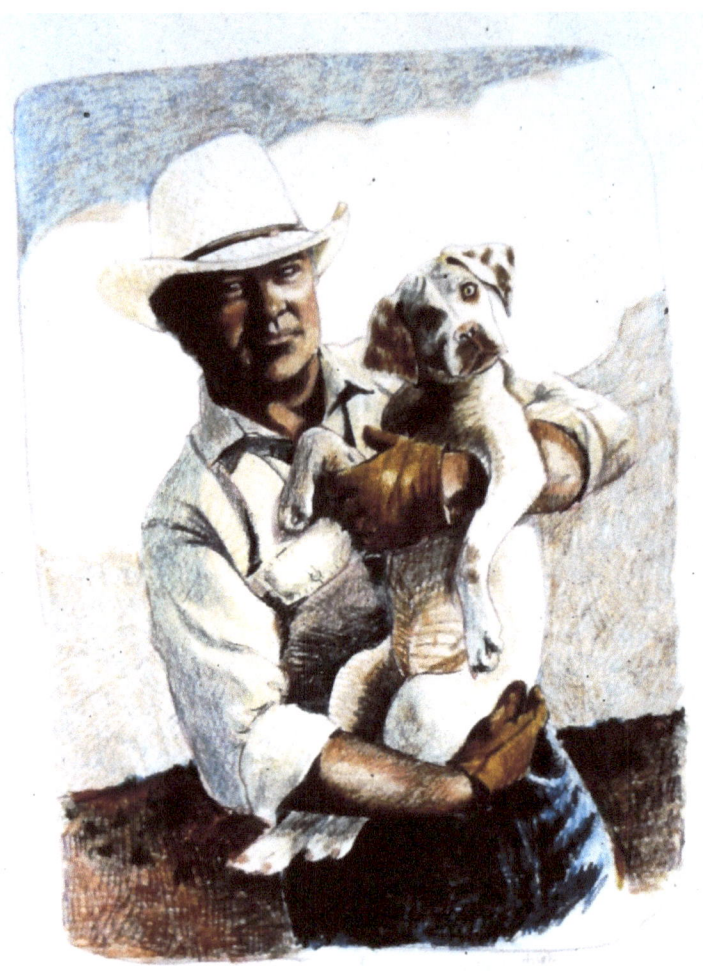

Cowboy & Dog, date unknown, colored pencil on paper

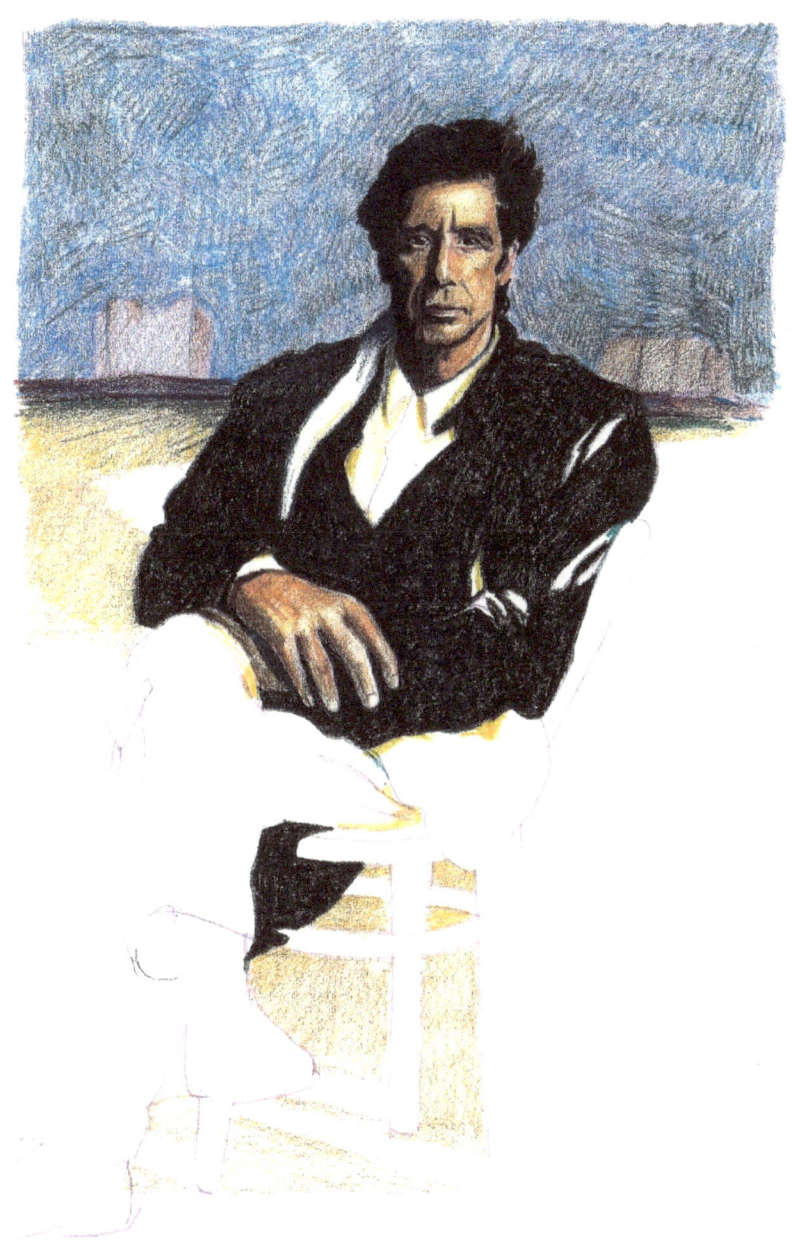

Al Pacino (unfinished), circa 1989, colored pencil on paper

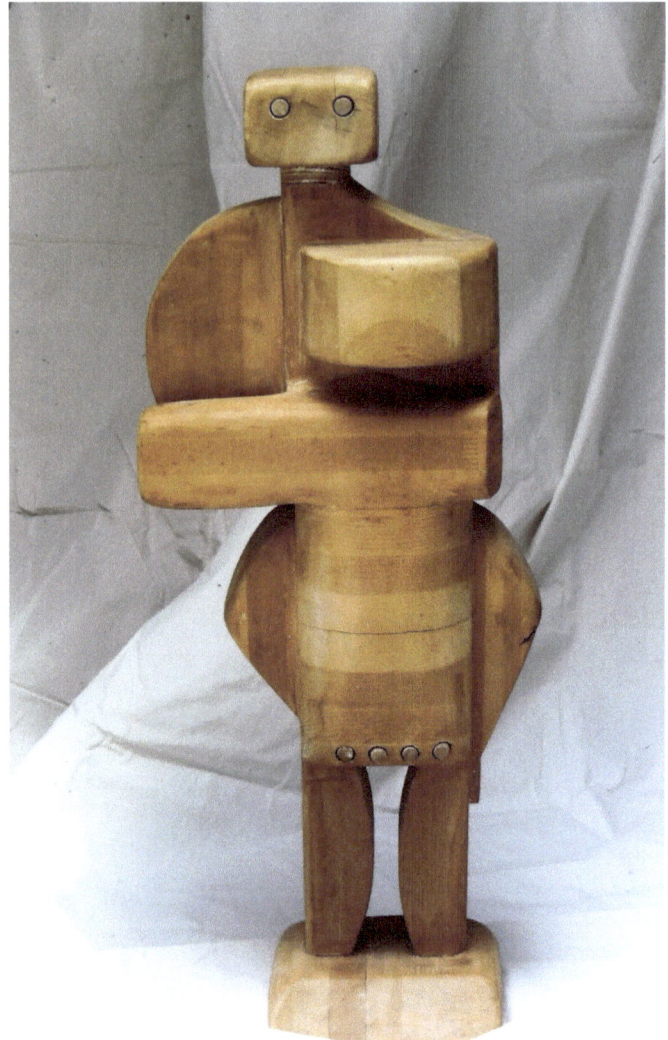

Future Man, circa 1969, sculpture in wood

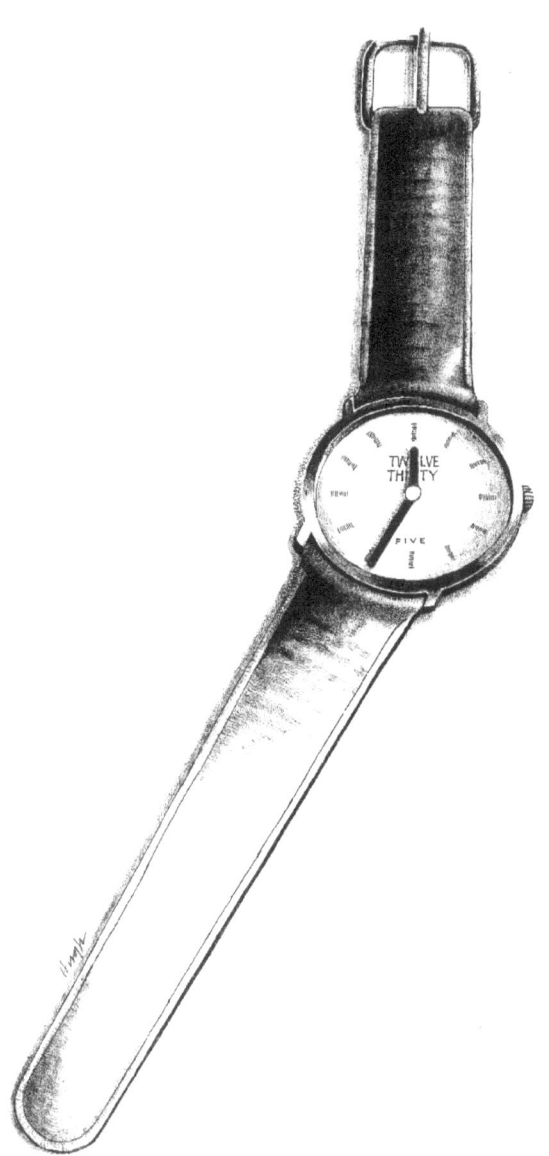

Untitled drawing, date unknown

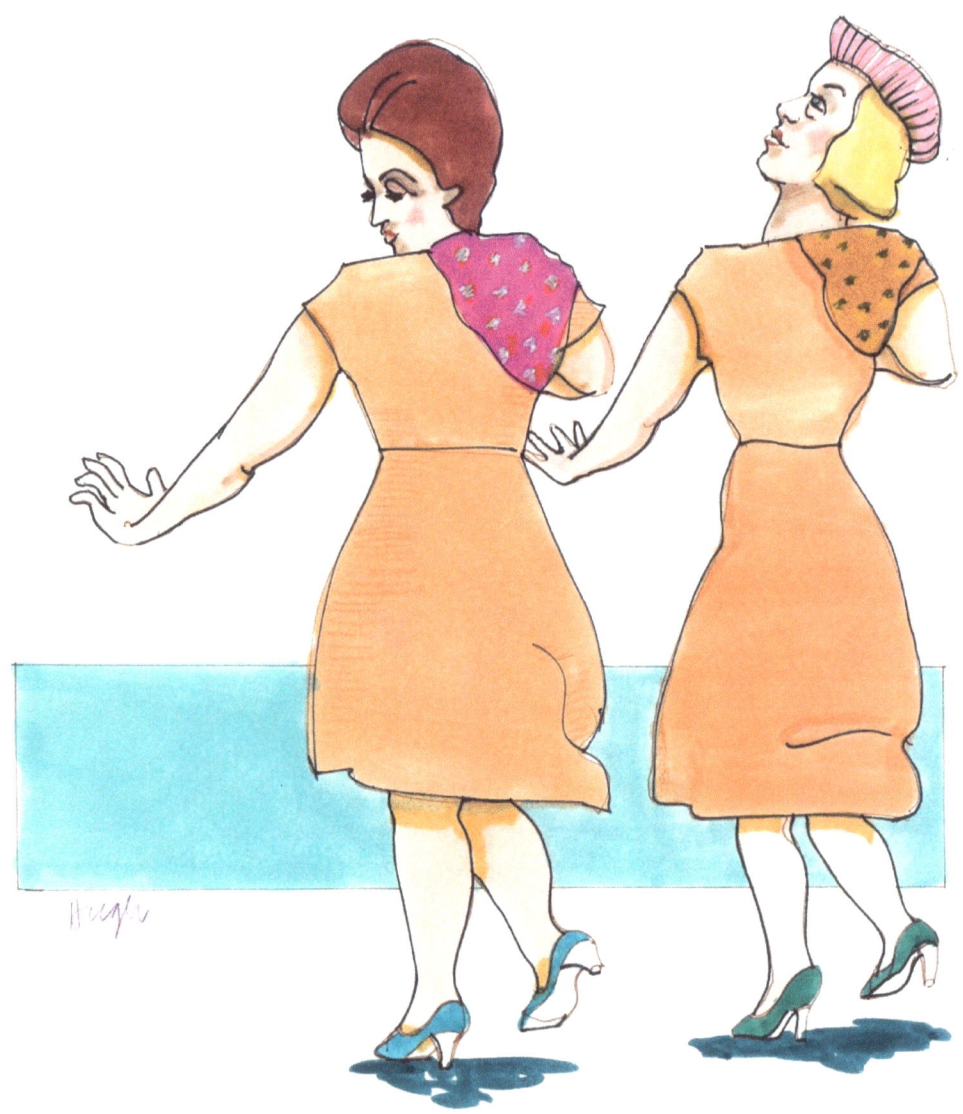

Stewardesses, date unknown

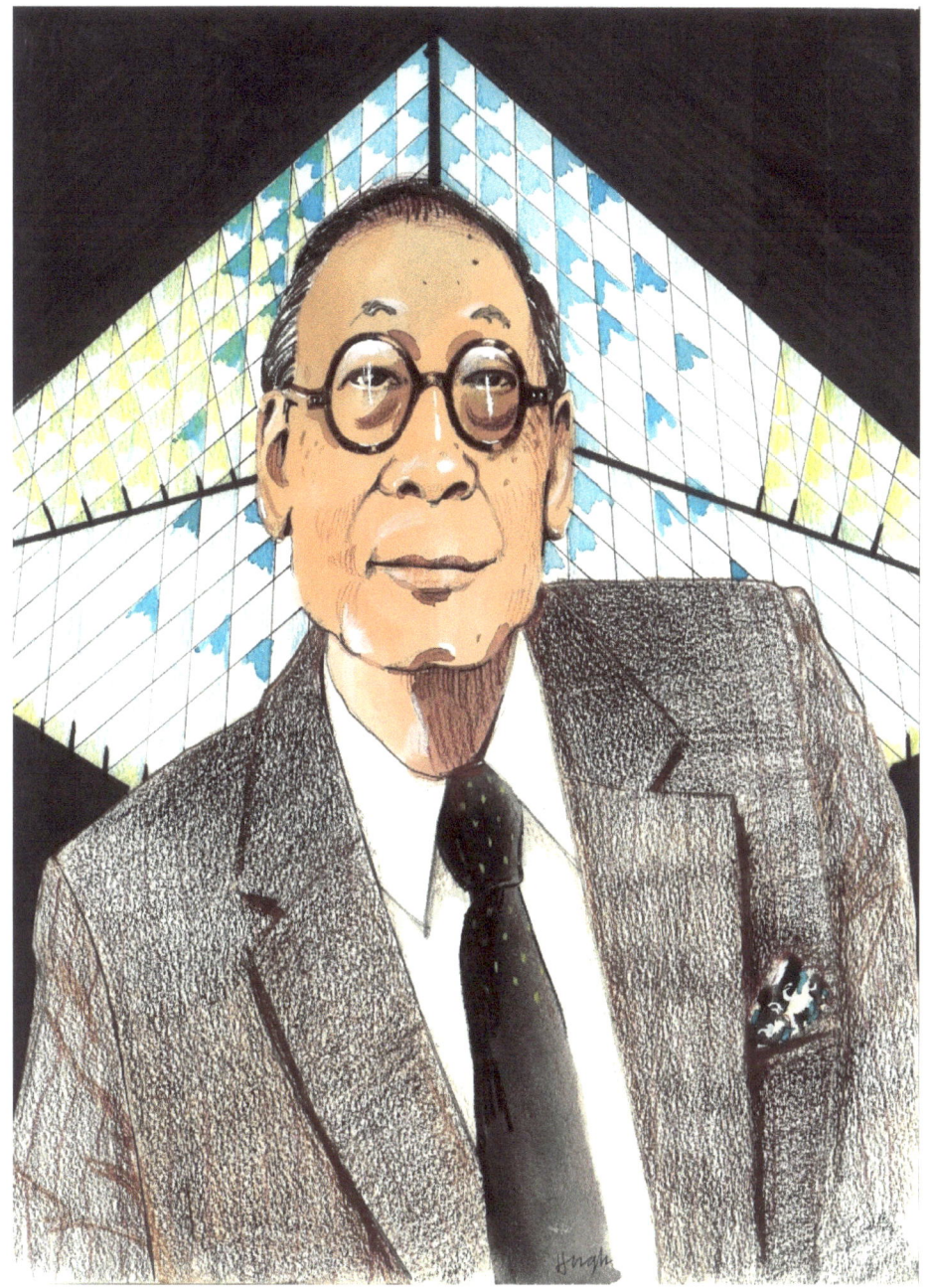

Business Man, date unknown, colored pencil

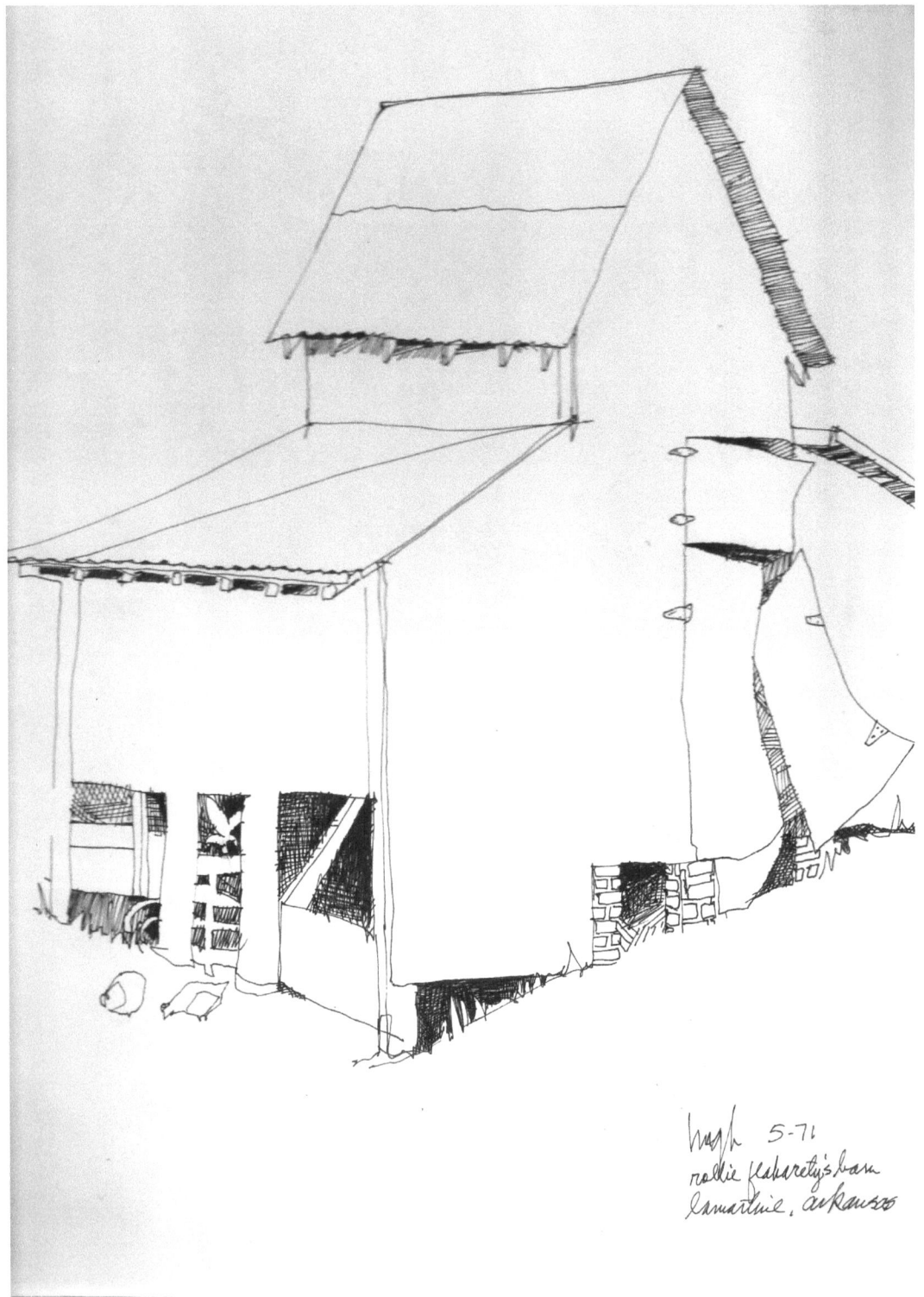

Flaherty Barn, 1971, ink on paper

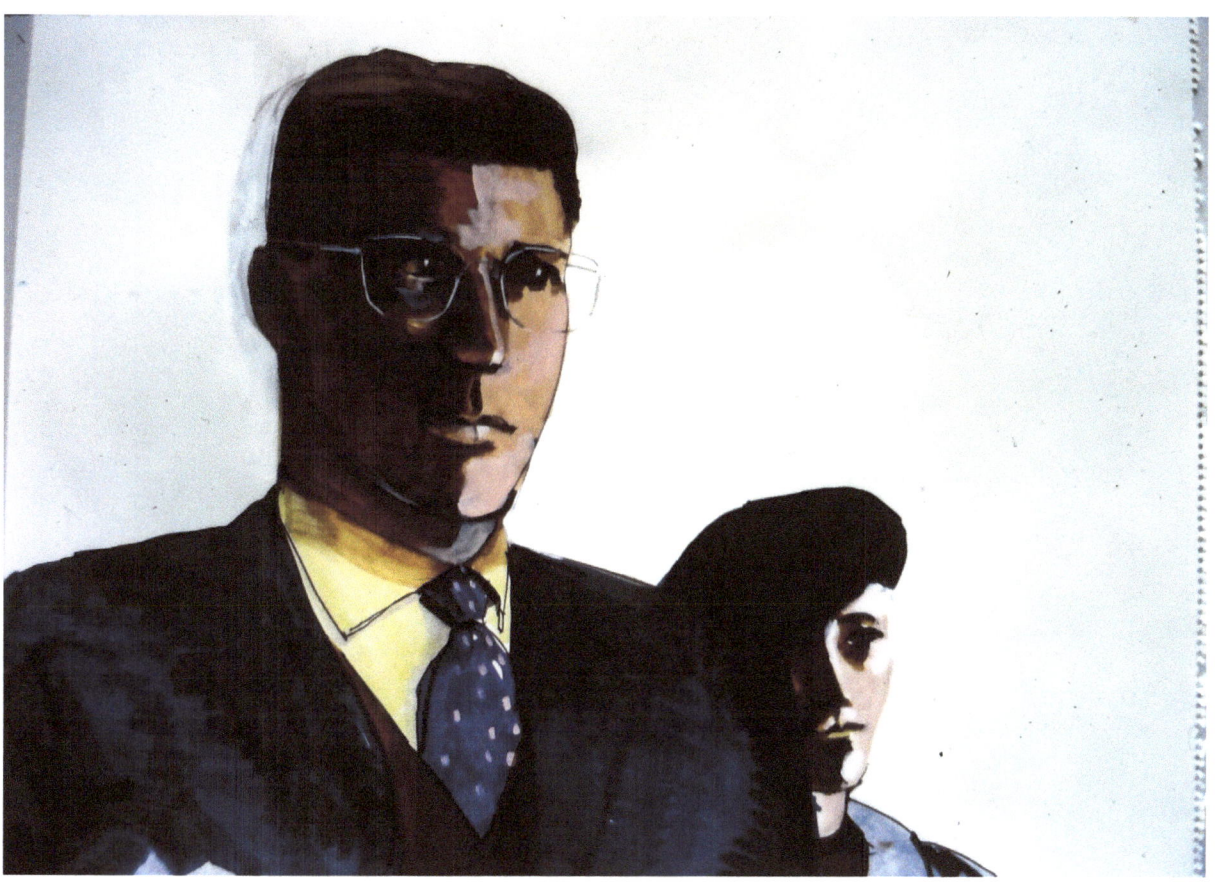

Untitled drawing, date unknown

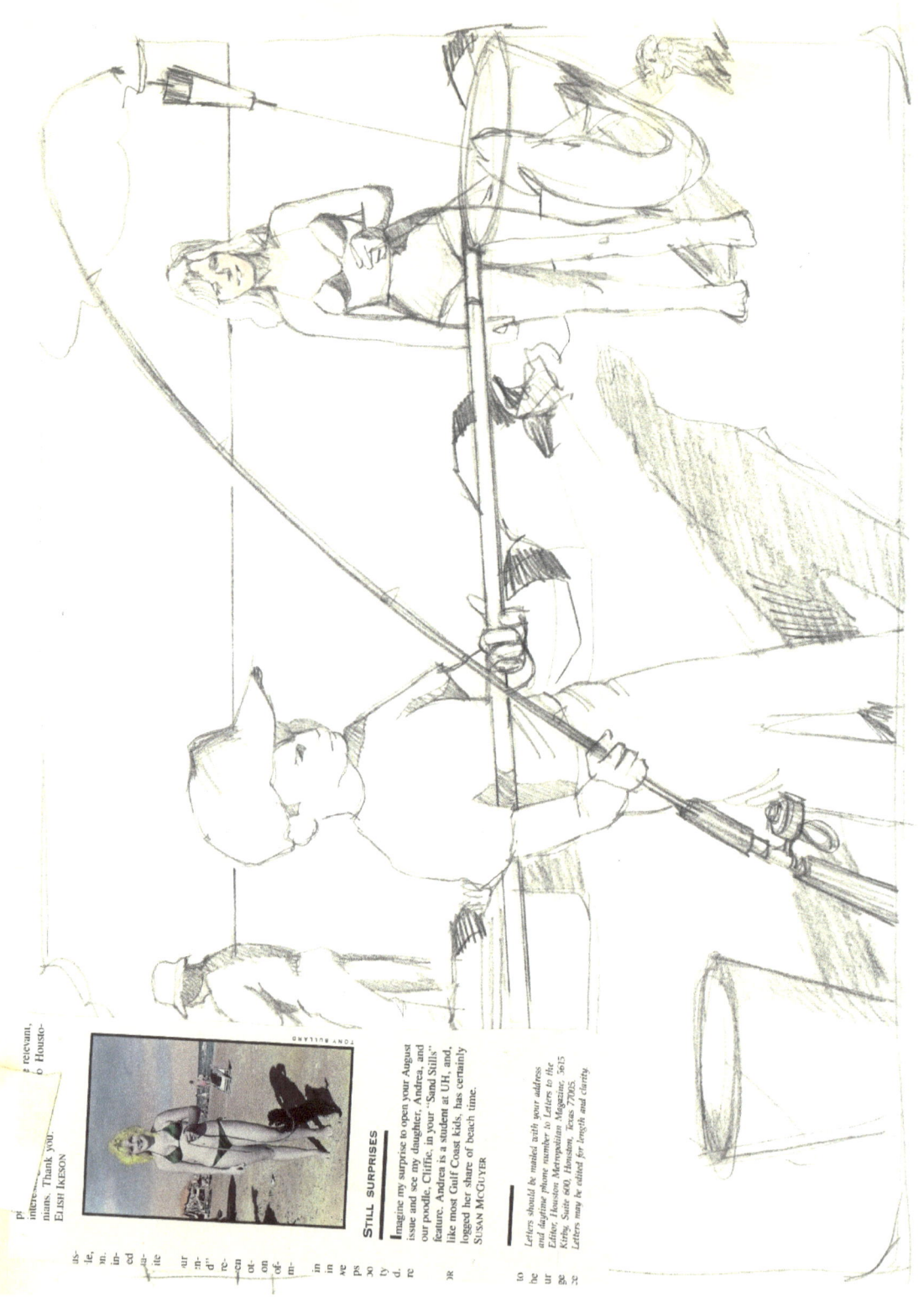

Unfinished drawing (and inspiration), date unknown

78

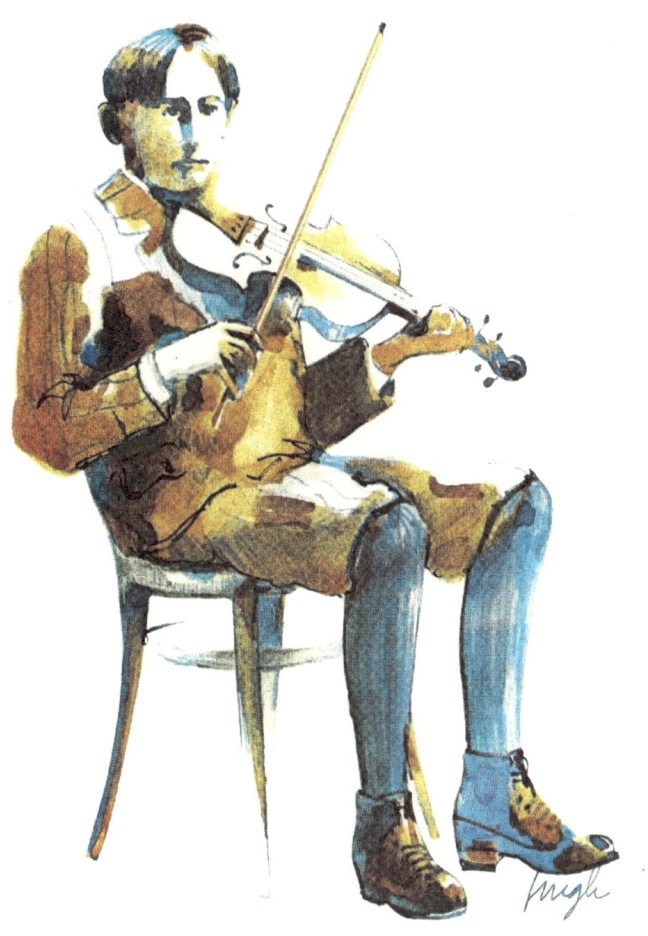

Illustration for magazine cover, 1972

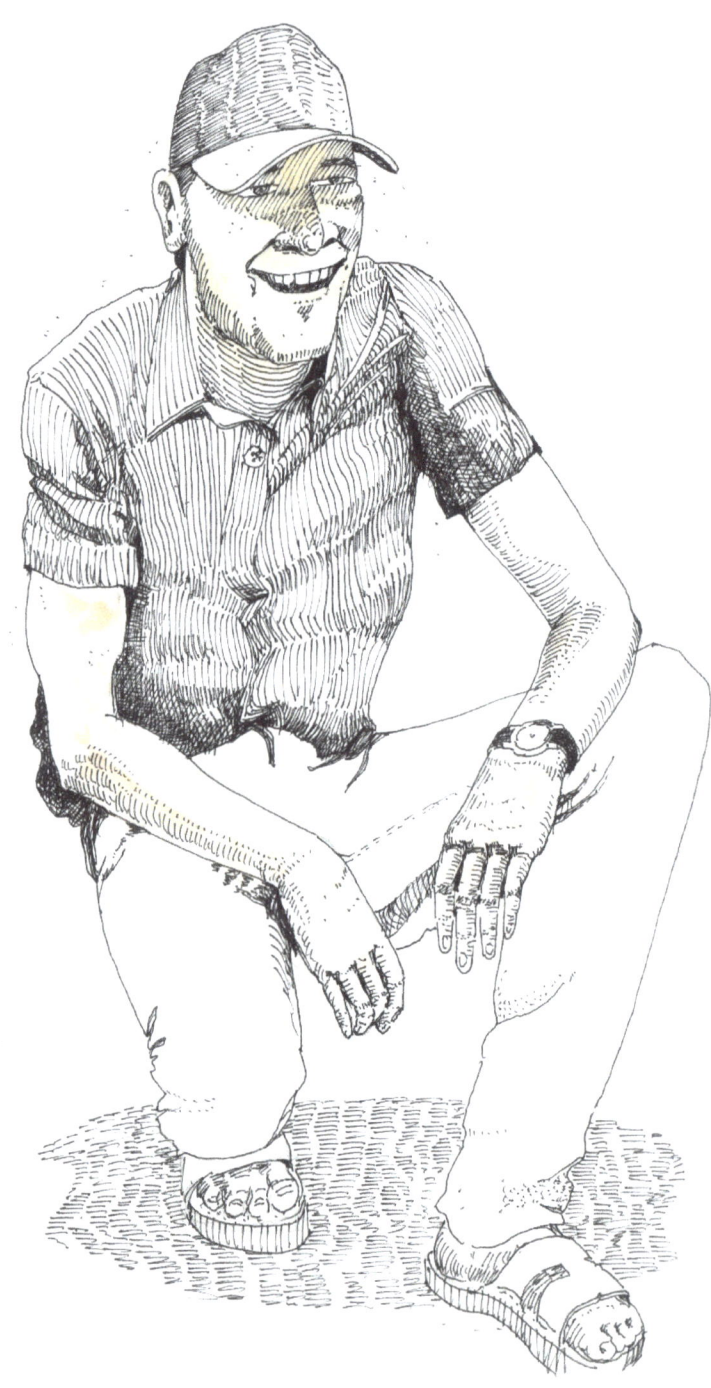

Untitled Drawing, date unknown

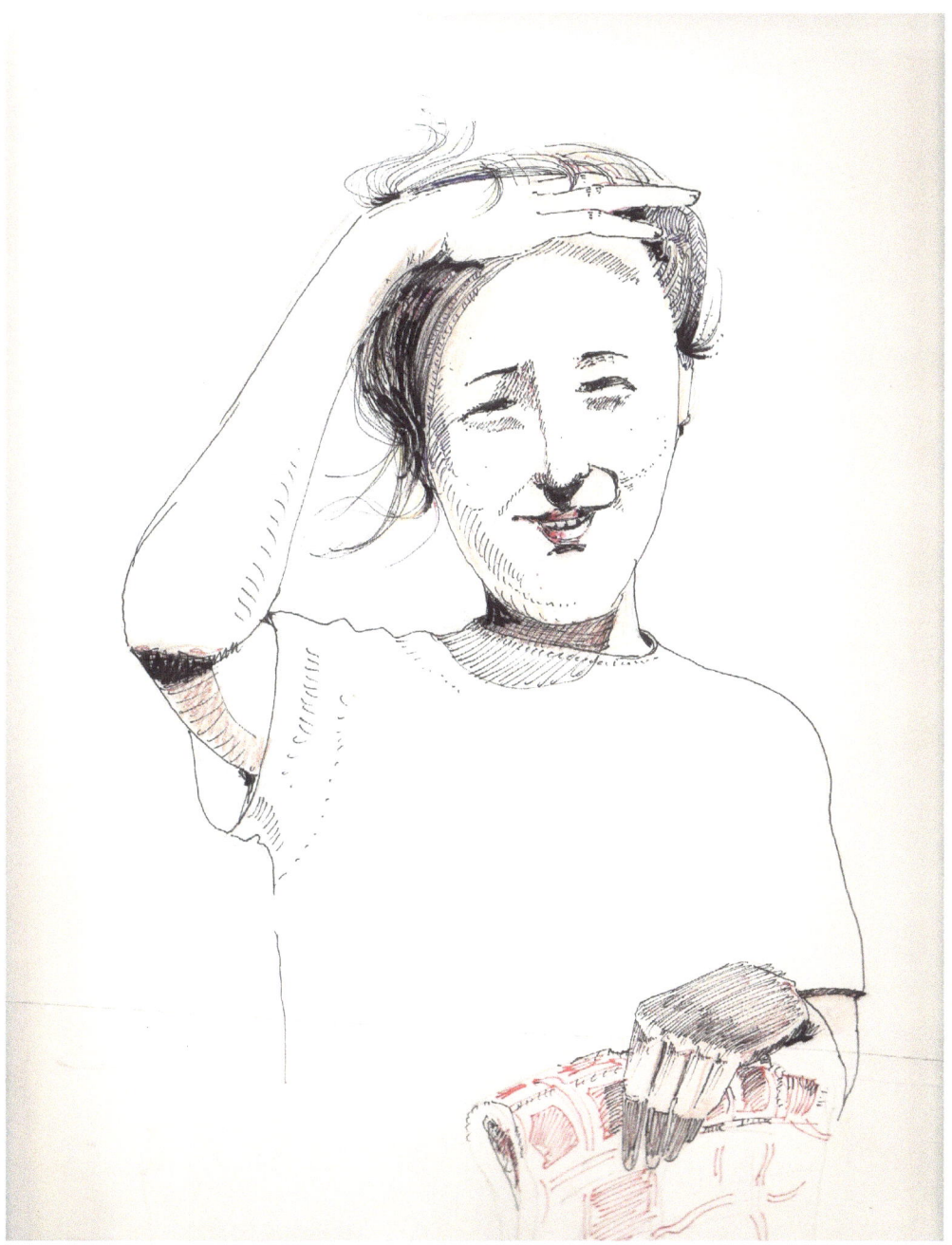

Untitled drawing, date unknown

About the Artist

Hugh McDonnold, Sr., Texas artist and ad-man, was born near Houston in 1939. From an early age he loved drawing horses and cowboys. In summers he spent time working on his cousin's cattle ranch in Liberty County, living the life he had earlier drawn. In high school he rode the Salt Grass Trail, a cattle-drive reenactment beginning in Brenham and culminating in the parade that opens the Houston Livestock Show and Rodeo. Graduating from San Jacinto High in 1957, McDonnold's life took him to Texas Tech University and the U.S. Marine Corps Reserves before finishing a degree in fine arts at Sam Houston State University. After that he returned to Houston with a young family and began a career in advertising. In 1990 he left it to do freelance work and paint. He exhibited in many shows and galleries, and the beauty of natural places—oceans, prairies and hills—figures prominently in his work.

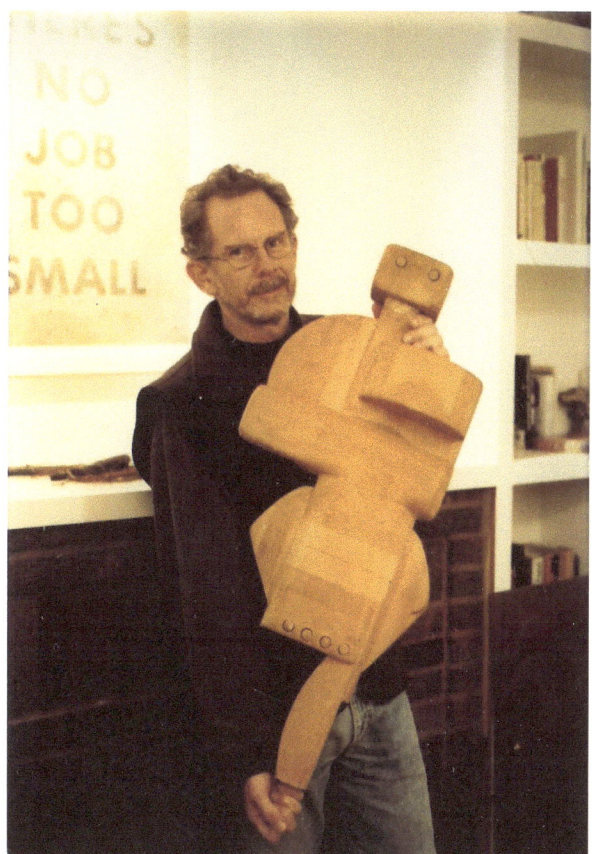